To Nana

MW00769548

The LAND
of
Plenty

A Soulpreneur's Guide to Finding JOY, POSSIBILITY, and ABUNDANCE through Money Empowerment

CAROLYNN BOTTINO

Abundantly & Joyfully —

Carolyn Bott

THE LAND OF PLENTY

© 2019. Carolynn Bottino. All rights reserved.

Money Empowerment Press
www.moneyempowermentproject.com

ISBN: 978-1-7341796-0-6
Library of Congress Control Number: 2019917049

Photography: Jill Fleming Photography
Cover design: Carolyn Sheltraw Graphic Design

Disclaimer: Some names and identifying details have been changed to protect the privacy of individuals.

Printed in the United States of America.

*Dedicated to you, the soulpreneur
who longs to find joy, possibility, and abundance.*

CONTENTS

INTRODUCTION

Money. It is a big topic. It is part of your life, every single day. It's something everyone wants more of. Yet, so many people don't want to talk about.

At this moment, you may be exhausted from working too hard, never making enough, wondering if you should even close your business. You may have no clue how much money you have made, or maybe you don't want to know for fear of seeing how much money you have lost. You may perceive yourself as poor, or a "starving artist," or someone who just isn't "good with money."

You may not be valuing your services, and pricing yourself in a way that doesn't support you.

Regardless of where you are and whatever labels you identify with, I'm glad you're here. This book will help you understand your money stories and money blocks, as well as your money patterns. It will give you practical ideas and empower you to understand your numbers. If you are open, this book will transform the way you think about money so you can live in what I call the **Land of Plenty**.

I believe the Land of Plenty is a place ALL of us can find. I dream of a world where all of us live here, all the time. Where you know without a shadow of a doubt that there is plenty of money. Where you aren't afraid you will run out of money or there won't be enough. Where the show isn't run by greed or fear. Where people support each other's businesses in micro-communities in which money quickly and easily regenerates and multiplies.

And where everyone knows that money is infinite.

I know what is possible with money. I have witnessed it with clients, and I have lived through my own money trans-formation. I will be sharing many of the details in this book of how it all unfolded. I can honestly say I am living the dream and I am abundant and joyful with money. I am not saying this to brag; I just know it is possible for ALL of us.

This book is not about budgeting or sales or investing. It's about soul work—and taking a journey to unleash the beau-tiful, magical, conscious soul of abundant money that I believe lives inside each one of us.

Consider this book your invitation to:
- break through and embody joy and abundance.
- understand where you have been and where you want to be financially.
- work on your money mindset and money mindful-ness.
- recognize where you are feeding into fear and scar-city.
- transform your life, so you live in the Land of Plenty.

And it's for you if:
- You identify as a Soulpreneur (an entrepreneur who runs your business with your heart and soul and lives out your soul purpose through your business).
- You are open to being magic around money.
- You are looking for a holistic approach and practical advice with a bit of emotional and spiritual work thrown into the mix.
- You hold the possibility that the Land of Plenty exists (even if you aren't into "woo").
- You're ready to learn about money in a whole new way.

This book may not be for you if:

- You want a quick fix for your money problems. Newsflash: You aren't broken. There is nothing to fix. This book is about seeing your money through a lens of *possibility*, not brokenness.
- You want a step-by-step guide or formula to get your business to six figures in six months. This book is a deep dive into your money stories, blocks and patterns; it is not a one-size-fits-all, get-rich-quick kind of book. (Though if you happen to get rich after reading it, I'll be the first one to celebrate with you!)

Before we go any further, I want to assure you of something: I approach money with zero judgments. Zero. Zilch. Nada. Judgment feeds into fear and scarcity and it doesn't have a place in the Land of Plenty. Whatever your money story is, it's OK. I've seen it all.

Also, you might think money books are boring and written by stuffy know-it-alls who shame you for not having more in your retirement account. Please know this book is not that. Not that AT ALL.

So, what made me write this book? I am a bookkeeper, but I'm not your average bookkeeper. I don't own a suit and I spend most of my days in jeans. For the past six years, I've lived and breathed other people's money, but I'm not interested in telling you what you should be doing or how you should be doing it or giving you a formula to follow. I'm just ready to share the wholehearted wisdom I have collected after spending a lot of intimate time with people and their money.

I am no money guru. I simply believe that money is a tool to support you in your life's desires and I believe the Land of Plenty is real.

Finding the Land of Plenty

There are three steps to finding the Land of Plenty:

The first is **exploring your money story**. Every single one of us has a money story. This book is just a piece of mine, and throughout the pages I will be sharing lots of juicy details from my life, along with the money stories of my clients and others I've observed. You may see yourself in these stories. It is surprising how common some of them are, but they are just STORIES. And they can be re-written into new beliefs and patterns. No matter where you are right now, you have a choice about how you interact and feel about money.

Second is to **make some deliberate choices and take action to create abundance**. Here is where all the practical pieces fall into place. Once you see what you want, you can take action and create systems and patterns that help you feel less stressed around money. Stress repels money. The more you chase money, the more it runs. Deliberate choices allow you to live a life of joy and abundance.

The last is to **unlearn what has been holding you back and break through to your money transformation**. Transforming your relationship with money does not happen overnight. You have to be willing to open yourself up to receiving everything you are asking for. And many times, it doesn't show up the way you think it will.

Finding the Land of Plenty is a journey and it happens one breakthrough at a time.

Money Breakthroughs

Writing this book has been magical, which leads me to believe that it will be magical for you, the reader, as well. When my editor, the wonderful Madeleine Eno and I sat down in late 2018 to map out the contents of this book, I drew three cards from the Osho Zen Tarot deck. I drew a card for me as the author, a card for the writing process, and a card for the book. The card I drew for the book was *Breakthrough* and it included a message that I knew was for you, too.

> *If you are now feeling that "enough is enough," allow yourself to take the risk of shattering the old patterns and limitations that have kept your energy from flowing. In doing so you will be amazed at the vitality and empowerment this Breakthrough can bring to your life.*

You may be feeling that enough is enough around your money. Are you ready to shatter your old patterns of limitation? Are you ready to rise up and be empowered around your money? Are you ready to feel joyful and abundant when you think of money?

How to use this book—At the end of each chapter you'll find a list of Money Breakthrough questions. I encourage you to dedicate a journal to use as you read this book. Spend some time contemplating and writing your answers to these questions.

Money breakthroughs happen in baby steps. Each time you answer a question, it is a baby step. If you don't know how to answer a question, that's ok. There are no bonus points for answering them all. Answer what is speaking to your soul at this very moment. Some of the answers will be obvious to you, some of them might show up days, or weeks, or even months later.

Just a word of advice. The topic of money is HUGE and full of emotional triggers.

Be gentle on yourself—it's a process and a journey, not a race. Stop judging yourself and your current relationship with money. If you need to read one chapter or even one section and take some time to let it sink in, that is totally ok.

Believe me, your shit can come up when you start working with money, and it's very easy to zone out. I invite you to take the time you need to stay with it. *Breathe.* If something is coming up, that means you are ready to look at it. Just come back when you are ready because every single chapter and section brings you one baby step closer to living in the Land of Plenty.

By picking up this book, you're already way ahead of most people who prefer to keep their head in the sand around money. If you slow down and give the breakthroughs time to settle in, you'll have the space you need to shift and transform. Remember, breakthroughs come from paying attention and *doing* something.

Messages from the Universe

The Universe conspired with me to write this book.

Every day I hike the trails in my San Diego neighborhood and as I was writing this book, I listened for the whisperings of what needed to be written. When I got home from my hike, I sat down at my desk and let the words pour out onto the page.

The Universe asked me to step up and write this book. But more importantly, I *listened* to what the Universe was asking of me. As you sit with the questions at the end of each chapter, I invite you to listen to what the Universe has to say about your money. More than anyone or anything, the Universe has your back and wants you to have joy and abundance in your life.

There are no accidents. The words I have written on these pages contain the message you need to hear right now at this very moment in time about your money. Although I am writing this book in 2019, you may be reading it in 2020, or even 2040. I promise you the messages you receive from this book are what you need to hear at the very moment you are reading this book—if you are open to receiving it.

I know three things for sure.

1. Money doesn't have to be scary; it can actually be joyful.

2. Money is infinite.

3. There is a world of joy, possibility and abundance and it is called the Land of Plenty.

Ready to join me there?

Part One

Exploring Your Relationship with Money

Chapter One

How Your Money Story Is Holding You Back

I was born in middle America in the middle of the 1970s to a middle-class family. Looking back, I realize with a huge amount of gratitude, that I was born into a privileged life. We weren't poor and we weren't rich, but I never worried about where my next meal was coming from, and if I had clothes to wear or a bed to sleep in each night.

I lived a pretty sheltered life as far as money was concerned. Our neighborhood was nice, all the kids played outside well after dark, we walked to and from school without any adult supervision, and within my elementary school, I certainly didn't recognize anyone as being "poor." I didn't really think about money or feel stressed about it. Somehow, I knew it would always be there when I needed it.

The first time I remember my parents talking about money was when my mom and stepdad were getting married and buying a house. Combining our families meant there would be four kids plus my parents in the house—and they wanted us each to have our own bedrooms. It was the early 1980s and interest rates were crazy high. I later learned they had financed the house with a balloon payment—a short-term note that had to be refinanced or paid off within a couple of years.

Bottom line: They were "house poor." All their money went to the mortgage. I remember not having any furniture in the living or dining room for quite some time, and the very old, ugly, orange and brown floral couch that dominated our family room well into my teenage years.

While I don't have any recollection of my parents arguing about money, on some level I could feel it in the air. Both of them worked really hard for every dollar they brought in.

My stepdad owned an electrical contracting company that he ran out of our basement. Every workday, a dozen or so electricians showed up at our house to check in and head out for their day. A secretary who answered phones and scheduled the crews worked from the basement. Around 4:00 pm, the crews returned and parked their work vans in front of our house. There was always a constant flurry of people coming in and out of the basement door.

My mom worked full-time as an executive secretary. She got home around 5:30 pm, cooked dinner, and after eating immediately scurried down to the basement, which also housed the second family business, The Robbins' Nest.

Somewhere in the mid 1980s, my industrious and crafty mom decided to put her talents to use and made a variety of hand-painted items that she replicated and sold in various shades of pastels.

This was long before the days of Etsy, and selling craft goods meant packing up everything you had spent countless hours creating, hauling it to pop-up craft fairs, setting it all up for display, selling for two or three days straight, and then packing up the leftovers at the end of a very long weekend. Many of my childhood and teenage vacations revolved around road trips in our motorhome packed with grid wall, six-foot banquet tables, and boxes and boxes of hand-painted goods for sale. I am sure Mom spent any vacation days from her "real" nine-to-five job working craft fairs.

One of the most inspired items she created was a rolling pin recipe holder. Picture a piece of wood handrail that was cut to six inches long, with two wooden beads that looked like rolling pin handles attached at either end. A slit in the top of the wood held a recipe card, and the front was painted with hearts, apples, or the saying: "Love is Homemade."

These little rolling pins turned out to be quite the rage among craft fair attendees and my mom jumped on the opportunity to supply the demand. Before long she was wholesaling them all across America, and the basement factory began.

The Robbins' Nest employed all of the neighborhood kids. Some worked in the garage cutting wood and drilling holes, others stamped the bottom with a copyright stamp, pounded dowels into the holes so bead handles could be attached, or dipped the rolling pins into a vat of sealant. By the time I was in 9th grade, Mom had trained me in the highest of arts: hand-painting the rolling pin patterns. The two of us, along with my cousin Shauna, painted for hours on end in the basement.

I painted rolling pins through high school and most of college. I was paid by the number I painted, so I learned to be very efficient. My hourly rate ended up somewhere around $12.50, which for a teenager in the early 90s was pretty impressive. I was making bank!

Then Mom came up with another idea for a craft product. The Imagination Stick was a long wooden dowel embellished with two long, colorful ribbons stapled together, taped to the top of the stick, then shredded into small strings. Imagine a thin, mini pom-pom with longer strings. As the name implies, it was great for sparking kids' imaginations and also made a pretty kick-ass cat toy. We sold them at the craft fairs for $1 each. Enter the next mass-produced product—but this one was all mine. After paying Mom a commission for each stick I sold to cover the cost of the materials, I could pocket the profit. Ka-ching!

When I was 15, my parents told me they would match whatever I could save to buy a car. By the time I turned 16 I had saved $1,500 and purchased my first used car for $3,000. Thanks to rolling pins and imagination sticks, I was living pretty large for a teenager. I had an incredibly impressive CD collection and paid my own way to Germany my senior year. (Now, *that* story would make an amazing book of its own!)

My friends perceived me as rich. I was often the one who paid for the movies, a night at the under-21 dance club, or the late-night pizza because my friends didn't have the kind of money I did. It's not like I was living a lavish lifestyle by adult standards, but by teenage standards I certainly was, and no one around me had the cash flow I did. I shared the wealth and gave away a lot—but I also set myself up to be taken advantage of by a few friends and dealt with my fair share of jealous mean girls.

I never really worried about the money running out or not having enough. Somewhere inside, I knew I could make more money any time I needed to, although I didn't quite have the words to express that.

Between watching my stepdad run his electrical business, watching my mom work a full-time job and run her craft business, and working in the craft business from a very early age, I learned a lot about business and money, and how to make money. I learned what it takes to be an entrepreneur. I learned to work hard, work fast, work efficiently, and never expect something for nothing.

And while these are all solid lessons and certainly have their place, I also took in the shadow side of these lessons, as we always do when we learn by example.

I learned you had to work hard—like REALLY HARD— to make money. I watched both of my parents work 50 - 60 hours per week or more, and work incredibly hard for every single dollar they earned. They never watched TV because they were always working. When would they ever have time to watch TV? (Maybe that explains why we had that old ugly orange and brown floral couch for so long—no one used it!) And I had no idea that passive income streams even existed, or how to create them.

I learned you had to work all the time—like seriously 24|7. My stepdad was always on call. In the early 1980s he carried a pager everywhere we went. He was one of the first people to purchase a brick phone when they came out and wore it on his belt, Every. Waking. Moment. The answering service would call him at 3:00 in the morning to go out on service calls. I don't remember a time where he wasn't on call or working.

I learned you had to trade time for money. Every dollar my parents earned was in exchange for time they spent generating money. It never occurred to me you could run out of time and therefore run out of your ability to generate more money. (I don't think anyone in their teens or 20s thinks about running out of time!) It wasn't until my early 40s that I learned this lesson.

I also learned about working on vacation. While we did go out of town pretty regularly, it wasn't to sit back and relax by a pool; on most vacations we traveled to craft fairs, or something related to my parents' work.

I seriously don't know how my parents did it without completely burning out. And maybe they did, and they just hid it well. Honestly, if I NEVER see another rolling pin recipe holder in my life, it won't be too soon. (Sorry, Mom!)

Why Your Money Story Matters

Here's the thing: **The stories you carry around about money influence just about every thought you have about money.** How you earn, receive, spend, manage,

7

save, and splurge is a result of your stories. They impact what you think of people who are rich, and people who are poor. Your stories also define what you think you're "worthy" of having.

The relationship we have with money is formed by the family we were born into; the neighborhoods we grew up in; friends we hung out with; and our own personalities and perceptions that make up how we interpret our experiences with money.

Just as siblings can be so alike or so different, each of us has a unique relationship with money that is not necessarily defined by the amount of money we have, the opportunities we have been given or denied, or the financial situations we find ourselves experiencing.

And no matter what your story is...
- You can choose to live an abundant life.
- You can choose to find joy in your relationship with money.
- You can choose how to interact with money.

By recognizing your stories, you take strength from the pieces of your past that are beneficial and unlearn anything that isn't serving you. Joyful money bliss can happen if you make a commitment to explore and understand your money stories, and consciously create a plan of how to interact with money, which transforms your money habits and patterns.

Throughout my life and career, I have been able to see firsthand how hundreds of people interact with money. Some good, some beautiful, and some sad, terrifying and hard. Money is a part of life. It is with us every day, in just about every transaction we encounter. And even if we are not actually exchanging money, there is an undertone of exchanging value and worth in almost every single thing we do.

The stories I share are true—and while I am telling them

from my point of view, each person has a unique way of looking at money. You might see yourself in some of these stories. You might relate to a particular story, or you might find yourself judging another—all of this is 100 percent ok. Acknowledge your reaction because it will tell you something about yourself.

One of the best things you can do for your relationship with money is to become conscious of your *thoughts*, *feelings*, and *reactions*. This awareness allows you to evaluate the root of your feelings and thoughts, recognize patterns, and consciously make the decision of how you want to shift the way you feel about money. The first step is to understand your money story.

Uncovering Your Own Money Story

So, where do you begin? Uncovering your own money story can be painful, delightful, triggering, and empowering all at the same time. Remember, this is deep soul work.

Brain Dump. One of the best ways to discover your money story is to do a brain dump of all of your money memories. Yup, just sit down with a blank piece of paper and start listing every single memory you have around money. You might recall the first time you talked about money with your family, things or sayings you heard as a child, a time when you didn't get what you wanted, or an experience of wild success. It can be something that happened decades ago, or just last week.

Don't judge what comes up—let it all flow.

When I did my first money brain dump years ago, I couldn't stop thinking about it. There were so many memories in my life that revolved around money. I started a page in my journal for memories and over the next week I kept adding to the list. I would be out on a walk, or in the shower, or driving somewhere and something new would hit me, as if

I'd opened the flood gates. Some bubbled to the surface after being completely forgotten for years. Some of my money memories were painful. Others were joyful and made me proud to think about how far I had come.

Look for Patterns. The next step is to look through your list for patterns. Are there certain feelings or reactions to money that keep coming up, or situations that keep repeating themselves? Where do you feel stuck around money? Are there money memories that are feeding into why you are stuck? Is there a story you have been telling yourself about your money that isn't true? Is there a belief around money that has been dictating your decisions that no longer serves you? Write it all down.

For me, it was blatantly obvious that almost all of my money patterns revolved around feeling like I had to work REALLY HARD in order to earn money. No surprise there, right? I had issues letting go of control. I constantly felt that if I didn't work hard to earn the money, I wasn't worthy of receiving it.

Keep in mind your money story is not linear. Something that happened last week could be as powerful as something that happened at age 10, and this in turn sheds light on something that happened when you were 20.

Own your story. Regardless of what comes up for you, know that your story is uniquely yours and uncovering what makes you tick around money is priceless. What happened in the past is what got you to this place—and here you are, ready to acknowledge what needs to be rewritten and move forward. No need to hide from your story or make yourself feel wrong for what you did or didn't do or have.

"Owning our story can be hard but not nearly as difficult as spending our lives running from it."
—Brene Brown

Why You Don't Like to Look at Your Money Stories

Money memories often involve guilt and shame. Guilt that you have credit card debt, shame that you don't have more money in your retirement account. Guilt that you haven't opened your bills in the past few months (or years), shame about not making more money.

In fact, guilt and shame are so deeply woven with money in our society that money is often a topic of fear, dread and avoidance. Talking about money is taboo.

But what if your relationship with money didn't have to be this way? What if you could stop judging yourself and leave the guilt and shame behind?

Money memories can trigger all sorts of emotions. This is about unpacking the baggage you may have been carrying with you for years (or lifetimes) without even knowing it was there. And don't worry if you don't have tons of money memories to uncover; even one or two is great.

You get to choose what is working for you and what isn't. You may discover that a story you told yourself about money is no longer true, or a belief you had about money belongs to someone else in your family. You may even see how your money story has shaped your life.

How Money Stories Influence Your Life

Just after college I got a job at a bank. I'd always enjoyed working with numbers and had a knack for balancing to the penny. I received my degree in anthropology with a minor in creative writing and had NO idea or plan for how that degree would make me money.

I was hired for $7.52 an hour. I worked REALLY HARD, of course. After about a year, I was up for a raise, but then my boss decided to leave the company and my raise got swept

THE LAND OF PLENTY

under the rug. I didn't have the knowledge or the courage to ask my new boss for the raise I had been promised. So, I continued to work REALLY HARD for another *year*, until my new boss finally gave me that raise. Kind of ironic that I was working with people's money all day long but didn't have the skills to talk about money when it came to how much *I* was earning.

Then I went into nonprofit and worked REALLY HARD for not much money because I was dedicated to the cause.

Then I went into the corporate world and worked REALLY HARD and got taken advantage of because I didn't know how to stand up for myself.

Then I went back into nonprofit and worked REALLY HARD and got fired because I stood up for myself.

Then I started a business and worked REALLY HARD and... you get the drift here. Sometimes the way we've learned to behave around money doesn't really get us where we want to be.

Honestly, I didn't start to unlearn working REALLY HARD until I was three years into my business—21 years after I graduated from college and entered the workforce. It took a wake-up call, a desire to have something different, and a conscious effort to make the shift.

Your money story is an extremely powerful, moving force in your life. Remember, to be empowered around money, you need to be aware of how your story is playing out in your life...all the time.

When I talk to clients about their money stories, one of the first questions they ask as they start to uncover something meaningful is "What do I do with this?" I tell them to simply acknowledge it at first. Recognize it for what it is and how it has impacted your beliefs and actions. Acknowledge any patterns your story has created in your life around money. Then, if you want to change the script, make a conscious effort to be and do something different. Educate yourself. Forgive yourself for mistakes you made with money. Forgive others for their money mistakes that impacted you. Empower yourself with the actions you take from now on.

Just because you have a certain history with money doesn't mean you need to play out the same story for the rest of your life. It's your choice; you can rewrite the story.

"Step out of the history that is holding you back.
Step into the new story you are willing to create."
–Oprah Winfrey

Money Breakthrough Questions

What are your memories around money? Do a brain dump and write out every memory you can think of. Don't judge anything that comes up. Let it all flow.

Do you see any patterns in your money memories? Do certain themes or thought patterns keep coming up that have defined or influenced your relationship with money?

What stories have you been telling yourself around money that are no longer true?

What beliefs do you have around money that no longer serve you?

How has your money story influenced your life?

What shift do you want to make around your money beliefs?

How do you want to re-write your money story?

Chapter Two

Perception Is Everything

Ever since I was in high school, I wanted to make a difference in the world. I was a teenager when the AIDS crisis was at its peak and I was passionate about sex education. There was so much fear and anxiety around sex. (Side note: There are lots of similarities between the taboo of sex and the taboo of money.) I grew up in Utah where abstinence-only education was the law of the land and the powers that be thought (and still to this day, believe) if you don't talk about it, kids won't have sex. BIG SIGH and eye roll.

In the late 1980s the government sent out a brochure to every household in the U.S. to warn people about how AIDS was transmitted. I had heard lots of things about AIDS. Most of it was misinformation about gay men and drug users who made poor choices and therefore deserved to have AIDS because they were "bad" people. No one ever told it to me straight. When I read the postcard and realized that anyone who was sexually active was at risk and finally understood what had been withheld from my "fragile and delicate" young mind, I got really pissed off.

Why would adults who were supposed to be guiding me withhold such important, life-saving information? This anger fueled me, and I spent much of my college years and beyond fighting for comprehensive sex education in the schools. (Interesting, our society doesn't teach money awareness in schools either!)

I had always wanted to work for a nonprofit that promoted sex education. I applied for a couple of jobs and was eventually hired by Planned Parenthood as the office manager and special projects coordinator, which basically meant anything that needed to get done fell in my lap. This included fundraising and event planning.

The board consisted of about a dozen extremely powerful and wealthy women.

This was the first time I had really spent any time talking to people about their money, other than giving out savings balances when I worked at the bank. I wasn't doing major donor development, but quite a bit of preparation went into asking for even the smallest donation. A few of the board members took me under their wings and coached me on how and why to fundraise. What was so interesting about this experience is that I saw what a difference it made to view money through the lens of abundance instead of scarcity.

These women were incredibly wealthy. They had lots of money, and they approached fundraising with an underlying belief that others had money to give as well. Rather than thinking "*This donor probably can't afford to give much, so I'll ask them for a small gift,*" they instead shared the mission of the organization, and why it was important to them. They extended the invitation for the potential donor to make a difference. There was no preconceived notion of what the donor could afford. The board members invited the donor to be part of something bigger. They empowered the donor to make the choice of how much to give.

They taught me that when you fundraise, you are giving someone the opportunity to support something they care about. As a community, together we can make more of a difference than you can as an individual. Donating to a nonprofit is making an investment in your community. Soliciting a donation for a nonprofit is not asking for a handout—it is an invitation and a gift for the potential donor to make a difference in their community in a meaningful way.

This idea blew my mind but made sense on so many levels.

It all comes down to perception. **How you *perceive* money makes all the difference.** Whether you are talking about fundraising, paying bills, buying a new car, or pricing your services, your perception shows up in your conversations and inner dialogues around money.

The Perception of Abundance vs. Scarcity

Though we live in a relatively wealthy country in the U.S., we're obsessed with scarcity. Think about it: We are constantly bombarded with images and stories of "rich" people who have it all and we are often led to compare ourselves, leaving us feeling inadequate, less than, and not enough. Marketing and advertising focuses on all the things we don't have but *should* want. It's really easy to compare what you don't have to what you *think* everyone else has.

Then there's the fearmongering. Everywhere we turn there are people talking about how there won't be enough Social Security for all of us when we retire, and how the next recession is just around the corner, and how the stock market is on the verge of collapse. And God forbid if you don't have two months' worth of living expenses in a savings account. It is so easy to feel terrified about your financial future.

What if abundance is simply a point of view?

People of all wealth statuses can feel lack or abundance. **Read that again**. It isn't about how much money you have in the bank; it is about feeling at peace with money. If you remember only one thing in this book, this is probably the most important. I have seen so many levels of wealth and poverty in my clients' bank accounts, but the bank balance has *no* direct correlation to how abundant someone feels. Zero. I have clients with millions in the bank who feel poor, and clients who are thousands in debt who feel completely rich.

17

Abundance is not a destination. It is a feeling.

For instance, I have two clients who are in very different situations. One is the heiress to a huge family fortune; the other has lived off less than $30,000 a year for decades. Interestingly, the one with the extreme family wealth struggles with scarcity. She is constantly worried about spending too much, paying her bills, and running out of money. The one who makes less than $30,000 a year very rarely worries about any of these things.

So, what is the difference? These feelings certainly don't correlate with the amount of money in their bank accounts. After working with both of them for several years I can confidently say it is *perception*.

Wealth really is a point of view. Each time we get a raise or start to make more money, that new level becomes our new normal. And when we make more money, our perception of how wealthy we *feel* rarely changes.

A large percentage of Americans identify as middle class, but have you ever really looked at the definition of middle class by dollar amount and compared where you stand? I read recently that 68 percent of Americans identify as middle class, while just over 50 percent actually make up the middle class.[1] The majority of Americans call themselves middle class because they think there is always someone who makes more and someone who makes less, so it seems like the label fits.

Are there places in your life where your perception of money and wealth have held you back from experiencing abundance? Are there labels you have identified with that are

---

[1] Northwestern Mutual's 2018 Planning and Progress Study, Web, 30 September, 2019 https://news.northwesternmutual.com/2018-09-25-Nearly-half-of-Americans-think-the-middle-class-is-shrinking-and-one-third-believe-it-will-disappear-entirely

keeping you in a box? What would be possible if you approached your finances from a place of abundance instead of scarcity?

When I first added bookkeeping to my list of services, I had no idea it would take me to where I am today. The journey has been beautiful, eye-opening and humbling all at the same time.

What makes me a great bookkeeper is that I am a puzzle solver—I love jigsaw puzzles and I have a superpower for seeing shapes and patterns and how they fit together. The more I expanded my clientele, the more I discovered similarities and differences between clients and their relationships with money. I started to see patterns around how people interacted with money, and since I am their bookkeeper, I also have the privilege to see how these patterns correlate to what is or is not in their bank account.

On the surface, I would have expected that the more money someone had, the better their relationship with money would be and the more abundant they would feel. This is not the case.

I have two clients who are mother and daughter. Let's call them Diane and Holly. Holly is the heiress to a family fortune I just told you about. They both come from generations of wealth and their inheritances would allow them to live lavishly without working a single day in their lives. From the outside you would never know they have this kind of money. They don't live in mansions or have private yachts; they live pretty ordinary lives. Based on their wealth status and similar money backgrounds, I would have assumed they would have very similar relationships with money, and very similar feelings of abundance.

I have worked with Diane for years. She is very generous and donates both time and money to causes she cares about. If she wants something, she buys it. She doesn't really pay attention to how much is in her bank account and what she is spending because she can always pull more money from other places when it runs out. It's not that she is frivolous; she just doesn't stress about the money.

Holly, on the other hand, is constantly worried she is spending too much. She works incredibly hard in her business to the point of emotional and physical exhaustion. Although she has the same financial means as her mother, she stresses over every single penny.

Having wealth doesn't necessarily translate into feelings of abundance. **To experience abundance, the perception of our money needs to be in alignment with our desires to have money with ease.** In other words, until Holly perceives herself as abundant, she will feel scarcity and fear around money.

Your Money Mojo

So, where do your perceptions come from? Why is it that Diane and Holly, two people from very similar backgrounds, with similar money stories, can have *such* different points of view about money and abundance?

My theory is that it goes even deeper than our stories. I believe that we embody energies that also have an influence on how we *feel* about money. This is what I like to call your **money mojo**.

After observing the patterns of lots of people around money, I discovered five distinct money energies that make up our money mojo. Think of them almost like chakras—each of us has all of these energies inside of us and when they are all in balance, money flows easily and the stress around money is minimal. But when we are at the extremes of these energies, abundance seems like a distant, unobtainable goal. We tend to be more joyful in our relationship with money, and certainly have less stress in our interactions with money, when our money mojo is in balance.

Wondering about your money mojo? Stop reading right here and go take the quiz at moneyempowermentproject.com. You'll receive your results right away. When you recognize your current money patterns, you gain critical insight into your relationship with money.

By *understanding* the lens through which you see *and feel* your money, a huge piece of your money story and money beliefs open up. This allows you the space to decide if the stories you have been telling yourself still serve a purpose.

The Five Money Mojo Energies

As you read through the various money energies, you will likely recognize aspects of yourself in all of them. Depending on what is going on in your life at any given time, you may feel differently or interact differently with money. By recognizing your current money patterns, you are able to make empowered decisions that help you to align your relationship with money in a way that creates abundance.

Free Spirit Energy

When I first met Alexandria, she was volunteering for a nonprofit to help plan a fundraising event. She was dedicated and passionate and always showed up to meetings excited and willing to give 110 percent. She was funny, personable, and intelligent. Her personality was electric, and I liked her immediately. She eventually asked me to help her get organized—not just with her finances, but with all the nitty-gritty details of her life. She was feeling overwhelmed and knew she wouldn't get her shit together without the accountability of someone looking over her shoulder.

Although we have been working together for several years, she rarely opens her mail; it just sits in a pile until she decides to throw it out without ever opening it, or I come by and open it for her. It's not that she doesn't have the money to pay her bills, and it is not that she is irresponsible (although some of you may have this judgment as you read

21

this description). She is what I call a *free spirit* when it comes to money. She doesn't really stress about money, but she also doesn't really pay much attention to it.

In general, people who are free spirits with their money often give of their time and resources without putting a monetary value on it. They tend to avoid thinking about or dealing with money and sometimes will bury their head in the sand when it comes to finances. They usually don't pay attention to money, but it is not necessarily because they don't have it, or they are trying to avoid it. It's just not that important to them.

Free Spirit Energy Strengths
- Gives freely
- Doesn't put monetary value on time and re-sources
- Not afraid to ask for help around money
- Doesn't have a lot of money stress

Free Spirit Energy Shadow Side
- Avoids thinking about money
- Buries head in the sand and is usually unaware of what is in bank account
- Usually lacks systems to help manage finances

Balancing the Free Spirit Energy
If you see yourself in this description and want to attract more abundance, start by simply **paying attention** to your numbers. Take baby steps: look at your bank balance, get a system in place to help you track your income and expenses. If that feels overwhelming, think about hiring someone to help you. Knowledge is power and you don't need to be afraid.

Spending Energy

My friend Nicole is one of the most generous people I know. She is always buying thoughtful gifts for her friends and family and wants to make every occasion special. Her UPS driver knows Nicole by name because he usually has two or three boxes to deliver to her doorstep every day. Her closet is full of clothes that still have tags on them. She loves to dress up and go out to dinner at least a few times a week, and her shoe collection might be the best I have ever seen. She loves to entertain and throws some epic parties.

Nicole's creativity is off the charts and everyone who comes to her house is welcomed with a warm hug, a beautiful spread of delicious treats and a never-ending glass of wine. Her kids have everything they could ever want, and every child in the neighborhood can't wait to get an invite to her kids' birthday parties. The last one had a cowboy theme and included face painting, a bouncy house in the backyard, pony rides, and an appearance from two "real" cowboys who roped and had a shoot-out in the driveway. Needless to say, Nicole's parties are always spectacular.

People who are spenders enjoy rich, lavish things and can be seen by others as extravagant. They are also some of the most generous people and put their money into causes and people they care about. They always want to help others and often show their affection through gifts. They are the first to pick up the check at dinner with friends. They sometimes live beyond their means. Spenders rarely focus on how they earn or receive money.

Spending Energy Strengths
- Generous and thoughtful
- Makes every occasion feel special
- Loves to entertain and be the life of the party
- Shows affection through gifts

Spending Energy Shadow Side
- Can be seen as extravagant or frivolous
- Doesn't put much energy into receiving or earning income
- Sometimes lives beyond their means

Balancing the Spending Energy
If you see yourself in this description and want to attract more abundance, know that it is ok to spend money, but also remember to **focus on how you earn or receive money** as well. Ask yourself if the thing you are about to buy will bring you joy. If it doesn't, don't spend the money.

Manifesting Energy

My good friend and client Cheri loves to travel. She has checked off most of her bucket list destinations around the globe. She owns a consulting business and has no problem finding clients because people are instantly attracted to her. Every time we go to lunch, she tells a new story of being in the right place at the right time—from finding the perfect dress on sale for 75 percent off, to having a friend who just happened to have an extra ticket to a concert she wanted to see. She always ends up with a great deal of free stuff, and trusts she'll always have enough money or be able to make whatever she needs quickly. Years ago, she bought stock in a small startup that has since made it big, and she also received an inheritance when her favorite uncle passed away.

People who are manifestors seem to pull money and opportunities out of thin air. Their friends and family often see them as "lucky." They may get things for free or win contests they enter. They typically aren't worried about money because they know there's lots of it out there to earn. However, they often approach finances without a "plan" because they have experienced money showing up when they need it. They can get frustrated when they don't meet their income goals, but many times it is because they are not acknowledging other income sources.

Manifesting Energy Strengths
- Always at the right place at the right time
- Money shows up when needed
- Often seen as "lucky"

- Usually not worried about money because there's lots of it out there to earn

Manifesting Energy Shadow Side
- Often "wings it" with finances and very rarely has a budget
- Has hard time acknowledging everything received
- Thinks that items of value that were not earned (like free stuff or money from family) "don't count" as income
- Frustrated if goals aren't met

Balancing the Manifesting Energy
If you see yourself in this description and want to attract more abundance, be grateful for what you have and **acknowledge when money comes to you—in all forms**. Try tracking your income, including not only cash, but also other items of value and unexpected discounts to see how much is really coming in. You might be pleasantly surprised. Don't judge where your money is coming from, or value business income more than money you are gifted from family. All money is equal. When you ask the Universe to deliver, sometimes it doesn't show up in the most obvious ways. Look at your expenses once a month to get an idea where you are spending. You might realize there are ways to save as well.

Vacillating Energy

One of my besties, Sarah, loves spending time with friends, traveling and going to concerts—and when she can combine all three, even better. She has traveled all over the country to see her favorite bands. She has a thriving business that allows her the flexibility and the money to create her dream experiences. Every once in a while, she will pay for a friend to go to a concert with her because she really wants to share the experience, even if the friend can't afford the ticket price. While she loves every second of the trip, when it comes time to pay, she has a sinking feeling in her gut. She has the money, but the thought of depleting what is in her bank account gives her anxiety.

People who vacillate have a love/hate relationship with money. On one hand, they love spending it and giving freely. On the other hand, they often find themselves without money, feeling stressed, panicked and feeling guilty about the money they just spent. It seems like it is always feast or famine.

Vacillating Energy Strengths
- Love/hate relationship with money
- Enjoys spending money on experiences
- Generous

Vacillating Energy Shadow Side
- Love/hate relationship with money
- Feels stressed, panicked and guilty about money spent
- Feels like feast or famine

Balancing the Vacillating Energy
If you see yourself in this description and want to attract more abundance, **be gentle and forgiving with yourself**. Do some money mindset work to help you feel ok with *having* money. If you feel up to it, create a budget that includes a savings goal and simply pay attention to how close you are each month—without judgment (easier said than done). This will help you see patterns in your earning and spending and help you come more to center.

Saving Energy

My client Mary is a real estate agent and a numbers geek (my kind of girl!). She owns multiple rental properties and meticulously tracks every single penny spent on each unit in a spreadsheet. She sticks to a budget each month that includes not only her living expenses, but also funding several savings accounts. She opened savings accounts for her two kids the day they were born and religiously invested five percent of her earnings in the accounts each time she closed a deal. She has always dreamed about taking a sabbatical and living in Europe for a summer but has put off the trip because it seems so impractical to spend the money—even though she has it set aside.

People who are savers are usually very detailed and organized with their money. Although they have money in the bank because they have great saving habits, they worry a time will come when they won't have enough and can fall into scarcity thinking. I call them penny pinchers, and they are always looking for ways to save on expenses. Sometimes they are so focused on saving they lose sight on how to make money or waste time they could be earning money researching ways to save money. They very rarely go on vacation or splurge on nice dinners or spa days.

Saving Energy Strengths
- Detail-oriented
- Organized and confident with money
- Usually has savings accounts
- Knows their numbers

Saving Energy Shadow Side
- Has money but doesn't enjoy it
- Stresses about little things that don't matter
- Can lose sight of how to *make* money
- Doesn't follow dreams because they seem impractical

Balancing the Saving Energy
If you see yourself in this description and want to attract more abundance, **focus some of your energy on *earning* money, rather than worrying about how to save it**. It might feel counter-intuitive but give yourself the gift of a splurge without guilt. Set aside a dollar amount or percentage in your budget each month to spend on yourself for things you see as "frivolous." Get

that massage, order the nice bottle of wine on your anniversary, use the expensive linens you got as a gift. Part of attracting and feeling abundant is being able to enjoy the things that money can buy instead of living in a world of scarcity. Learn to trust yourself with money and acknowledge that you know what you are doing.

Understanding Your Money Mojo

Do you see yourself in any of these descriptions? Some of them? All of them? I know I sure do!

There have been times in my life where I can relate to every single one of them. Most of the time I see myself in the manifesting energy, although in times of stress I can lean toward the vacillating energy pattern. What is interesting to me is that these patterns have been with me my entire life. As I have gone through various jobs, opened my business, had lots of money or no money in the bank, I still experience many of the same emotions and patterns around my money.

It is completely normal to move through different energies as your perceptions and experiences with money change. It is also completely normal to come back to those familiar patterns—even when you have leveled up and moved on.

As with most things, acknowledging where you are is one of the most powerful steps you can take to start to change. There are no "good" or "bad" energies and we all have a little of each. Keep in mind, the shadow sides of each can hold you back from feeling abundant. When you start to see patterns that are supporting bad habits or behaviors you want to change, being able to name them helps you recognize what is happening. When you understand your money mojo, you can also call in the energies you need to help balance the flow.

We each have a sweet spot where the magic happens. When I am in my zone, new clients seem to come out of the woodwork. I manifest unexpected gifts and lots of opportunities. When I am not in my zone, I spend money like crazy and then feel guilt and shame for not having more money in my bank account.

When I see this pattern cropping up, I stop and acknowledge what is happening in my life and what needs to shift. More often than not, it is actually my perception of abundance.

Let me explain. Recently, my husband sold his business. For months after the sale, I continued the same pattern of putting a certain dollar amount into our house savings account to pay our bills, although he no longer had a regular paycheck, and the way money was coming into our lives had changed drastically. For months, it felt like feast or famine (aka vacillating energy). One month, we'd have lots of money in our bank account, and then in a few months it would be gone and I would feel horrible, thinking I should have been better at budgeting and spending. I felt fearful and guilty and judged myself for not being better with money.

When I finally recognized this energy for what it was, I sat down and reworked my system around how and when we paid bills. All of a sudden, a huge cloud of fear lifted. The dollar amount that we had to work with was exactly the same—it was my vacillating energy that created a *perception* that was causing me to feel scarcity. By switching up my system to be more in alignment with my new reality I was able to alleviate some money stress and get back into the flow of feeling abundance. Within a week, I had three new clients.

Money Breakthrough Questions

What is your current point of view about abundance?

Where has your perception of wealth held you back from feeling abundant?

Are there labels you have identified with that are keeping you in a box?

What would be possible if you approached your perceived wealth from a place of abundance instead of scarcity?

Which of the money mojo energies do you relate to the most? How do you see these energies play out in your day to day life? (Hint: if you haven't taken the quiz, go to: moneyempowermentproject.com to get your results.)

What can you do to balance your money mojo?

Chapter Three

The Money Taboo

Epic Failures in Negotiation

After I landed what I thought was my dream job working at the Utah AIDS Foundation, I began to feel an incredible amount of money stress. The ability of the organization to provide services depended on me, the fundraiser, to bring in the money. I felt like I had to raise money or people would die. How's that for pressure?

My nonprofit salary was rather small, so the money stress only continued in my personal life. I was running on fear and scarcity.

As much as I loved the work and feeling like I made a difference, the stress was too much. I decided I needed to look for another job. I moved to the corporate world, doing event planning for incentive trips. Between the salary, expected overtime, and bonuses, I would be making double and working a lot less.

I loved the new job—it was a perfect fit for my skill set. I gave 110 percent and worked REALLY HARD (yes, still!), and in return I expected the company would take care of me.

While being an event planner in luxurious hotels and cruise ships around the world *sounds* amazing, the reality is really long days—usually around 14 to 16 hours—often for seven days in a row. A typical workday went something like this:

5:00 am – wake up
5:30 am – greet hotel staff and make sure breakfast is ready and audio visual is set up for morning sessions
7:00 am – morning sessions start
9:45 am – make sure buses are in place to load for group outings
10:00 am – greet attendees and see them off on group outings
10:30 am – last bus departs
10:35 am – make phone calls to the transportation company to arrange a private transfer for the guy who forgot he needed to be in the lobby at 10:00 am
10:45 am – schlep all of the boxes from the storage room to the housekeeping staff so they can deliver turn down gifts in the evening
12:15 pm – go change clothes that are soaked with sweat from hauling all of the boxes
12:25 pm - frantically look for something to eat for lunch before greeting the guests returning from the group outings
12:30 pm – greet the returning buses and hustle everyone into afternoon sessions
1:30 pm – make phone calls to audio visual company because one of the microphones isn't working
2:15 pm - help attendee change his flight because a really important meeting came up that he can't miss at home
3:00 pm – afternoon sessions end; staff the hospitality desk until everyone is seated for the awards dinner that starts at 7:00 pm.
7:12 pm – last guest checks in for awards dinner
7:13 pm – find new DJ for awards after party because the original one just called and said he was double-booked and couldn't find a replacement
7:55 pm – greet the bartending staff and the new DJ to make sure they know where to set up the after-party
9:00 pm – after-party starts
9:25 pm – eat dinner leftovers in the hotel kitchen directly from the chafing dish because all of the

plates and utensils have already been cleaned up and none of the hotel restaurants are open this late
9:45 pm – check on the after-party guests, and politely decline to do tequila shots with attendees who are excited about winning an award
10:20 pm – help aforementioned guest who lost her room key
11:00 pm – after-party concludes
11:15 pm – set alarm for 5:00 am and fall into bed, ready to do the same thing all over again the next day

While the days were grueling, I loved what I did, and I didn't mind so much because the overtime pay was fantastic.

I had been with the company just over a year when I was out on the road managing a program in Europe. Because of this trip, I was missing one of our monthly corporate meetings. I received an email from my boss filling me in on the policy updates that were announced at the meeting.

"Effective immediately, all program managers will be salaried employees, exempt from overtime." *Say what?!?*

There was no adjusting our base salary to compensate for the overtime we were expected to work. It was the first time the corporate rug had been pulled out from under me. I felt betrayed. Shortly after, they also announced they would not be paying bonuses that year (although all of the programs were turning a rather hefty profit).

So, instead of making $50K plus, I was now making around $30K. These two corporate decisions cost me nearly half of my small salary. This was a really big deal.

How could they do this to me? I worked hard, so the company should REWARD me—not take away everything they had promised, right?

When I finally built up enough courage to go talk to the big boss, I walked into his office scared to death, with sweaty palms and a pounding heart. It was the first time I tried to negotiate for myself. And it was an epic failure. All the things I wanted to say didn't come out right. All of my reasons that sounded perfectly on point in my head landed flat. What I heard in return was, "We can't do that, because we would have to do that for everyone" and "We can't afford that." I left his office frustrated and on the verge of tears with not a single cent added to my salary.

It was very obvious based on the conversation that despite how hard I worked to make the company profitable, those profits were not being passed down to me. I was deflated. I felt as if they were taking advantage of me.

I started wondering why talking about money was so hard. I asked people for money all the time when I was fundraising, but when it was about *me* and *my* salary and *my* value, it was just So. Fucking. Hard.

And why was that?

Because MONEY is the Ultimate Taboo Topic

People often feel it is easier to talk about sex than it is to talk about money. But why?

We live in a society that puts money in the center of all of our transactions *but* tells us to not to talk about money.

Society tells us we should want more—a bigger house, a better car, more money, more clothes, more toys, etc.—*but* we also shame people who come across as "excessive" and "flaunt" what they have.

We live in a society that tells us we should save money and stay out of debt *but* doesn't teach the basics of money man-agement in school and offers credit cards to college kids at new student orientation, moments after they just signed on the dotted line for their student loans.

So many mixed messages. It's no wonder we all have confusion, guilt, shame, frustration, fear, anxiety, and avoidance issues around money!

If I took a poll, I am pretty sure 99.9 percent of people would say they feel uncomfortable talking about money on some level. Our society in general finds it impolite to talk about money in just about every situation.

Think about these unspoken rules:
- *Don't ask how much someone makes a year*
- *Don't ask how much someone spent on their new house or car*
- *Don't discuss salaries with co-workers*
- *Don't leave the price tag on a gift you purchased for someone*

And the list goes on and on. So, if not talking about money is the norm, how do we ever learn to negotiate salaries, set pricing as entrepreneurs, and talk about finances with our spouses? These are certainly not skills that are taught in our schools.

There is *sooooo* much emotion when it comes to talking about money. There is a fear of being judged for what you make, or how much you have, or how much you don't have. Because money is such an emotionally charged topic, it is taboo—something you aren't supposed to talk about. Because talking about something emotionally charged is going to rock the boat.

Unfortunately, *not* talking about money is also what often keeps us stuck. So where does this cultural taboo really come from?

The Cultural Root of Shame, Guilt, and Fear

It's always interesting when I start working with a new client. They often freeze up in fear as they share their bank statements for the first time, or it's months after our initial conversation before they say yes and start to work with me. They express guilt ("I'm not organized enough") or shame ("I'm embarrassed to let anyone else see what is in my bank account and my credit card balances").

Believe me—I get it. I have seen the full range of ugly emotions after working with hundreds of people and their money. I've also felt all of them in my personal life. There is no emotion or feeling around money that would shock me.

But where do these feelings of guilt, shame and fear come from? Sure, we all have our money stories, but these feelings are part of something much bigger. As a society, we have a collective belief about money that is intricately tied to the individual's value. The amount of money you make correlates with how you measure up in society, and in turn, determines if you are "enough."

Throughout history, there are thousands of examples of mixed messages around money.

> *The love of money is the root of all evil.*
> *Money makes the world go 'round.*
> *Blessed are the poor.*
> *Diamonds are a girl's best friend.*
> *He was a Depression baby.*
> *She was born with a silver spoon in her mouth.*

These stories have been woven into the fabric of who we are as a society. While we might not be conscious of how they impact us individually, or even the details of the stories, they collectively have shaped how society views money. And that view is complex!

In its purest form, money is a tool. It was created as a way to simplify the bartering process. It was, and still is, a piece of paper, like an "I O U," to exchange services. We have turned money into something much bigger. A false god. We have made cash king. We have let it define who we are as individuals and as nations.

I recently was in Italy and visited Assisi. I had been there 20 years before and remembered loving the quaint town with its steep cobblestone streets that meander throughout the walled city. As I wandered the streets while thinking about this book, I was fascinated with the story of the town's patron saint, St. Francis of Assisi, from a cultural money perspective. As the story goes, Francis came from a wealthy family. He gave up everything he had to live a life of poverty. His entire religious order was built on vows of poverty. In order to be closer to God, he promised to stay poor. Let that sink in for a moment.

While I certainly don't want to offend anyone who is Catholic, or religious, for that matter, this is just one example of how shame around having money is passed down from generation to generation. Without saying it in so many words, there's a belief that you won't find peace if you're wealthy and you won't go to heaven if you have money.

I know this is a very simplistic analysis of the story of St. Francis. Without going too deep into a debate about poverty vs. greed, I just want to show how these subtle messages can lead to a belief that money is evil—and having money becomes taboo.

Even if part of us dismisses them, these cultural stories and beliefs are ingrained in us, just as our personal money stories are part of who we are.

Greed is the Opposite of Plenty

Many religions speak about greed as the flip side of poverty. For me, greed is not a morally corrupt behavior, but one that comes from fear of scarcity. If you are worried you won't have enough, you start to panic and hoard whatever you can find. If you are worried you won't have enough, you make poor decisions about how you treat people. Greed shows up in competitive work environments where people use cut-throat tactics to get ahead at the expense of others, where employers take advantage of their employees, and where salespeople undercut their peers to make the next sale.

You can also see greed at work in our super-sized American consumerism, where people:
- buy things they don't need to fill a void
- buy things they don't need to keep up with others
- buy things they don't need to prove their worth
- buy things they don't need to show their love

If you are spending out of fear and buying what you don't need, or if you are taking advantage of others to get ahead at work, you may want to get to the heart of what "enough" looks like for you. The main thing to remember is this: There is a natural flow of money—and greed stops it cold.

How the "Upper Crust" Feels Guilt, Shame, and Fear Around Money

An underlying belief in our world is that rich people don't have money problems. And while it is true the rich people I know don't worry about how they are going to pay their bills, they certainly are not immune to feelings of shame and guilt. In fact, many times they feel ashamed or guilty that they *have* money.

One of my wealthy clients jokes about starting a support group for wealthy people because there is a huge amount of cultural shame in *having* money. There are expectations of rich people to "share the wealth" and regardless of how generous a wealthy person may be in charitable giving, they are often judged as greedy because of the money they have.

Guilt, shame and fear are common money emotions regardless of how much wealth you have or do not have. Shame can be felt not only because you don't have money, but because you have too much money. Regardless of how much is in your bank account, you can still feel guilty about not being good with your money and fear that you will never have enough or that you will mess up and lose what you have.

Lynne Twist talks about this in her book *The Soul of Money* (which might be my favorite money book of all time). People with money often have an immense fear of losing it. Often within wealthy families people are pressured to act a certain way in order to maintain the family status. This can lead to power struggles, betrayal, and dysfunctional family relationships.

Money feelings are the same for rich and poor alike, just two sides of the same coin. Having more money doesn't mean the money emotions go away.

Break Through the Money Taboo

What if we didn't have to apologize for having money, being rich, or wanting money? What would be possible if we were able to have open, honest conversations about money? How would our world be different if more of us believed money was a tool rather than something we had to stress about, work hard for, and hoard?

These are big questions. And, I believe, incredibly important ones that will help us reach the Land of Plenty.

When we *unlearn* what we have been taught, we can break through the money taboo. The more conscious we become about money—in our relationships and in our actions—we start to change not only our personal lives but the world around us.

There is a lack of money conversations in our world. For many women, the place this lack is most prevalent is in salary negotiations or pricing services. So many of us avoid asking for a raise because we are worried our boss will think we are greedy. As entrepreneurs, we price our services under value because we fear no one will pay the higher price. Those ugly emotions of fear, guilt and shame hold us back from having crucial conversations about money. The taboo of money keeps us silent when our boss passes us over for a promotion, or a client bullies us into a discount.

Your breakthrough starts with having the guts to stand your ground.
Your breakthrough starts with being aware of your own money triggers.
Your breakthrough starts with unlearning shame and guilt.
Your breakthrough starts with owning your value.
Your breakthrough starts with having open conversations.

I certainly can't say that I am a master when it comes to breaking through money taboos—God only knows I still have my own hang-ups, but I can say that once I learned to stand my ground and set some boundaries, things started to change.

The Ladies of the Literary Club

The last "real job" I had before opening up my business was running an historical event center. The building was owned by the city and operated by a nonprofit that saved historic buildings. It was a perfect fit and I loved my job.

After several years of successfully managing the event center, the nonprofit was gifted a second building by the Ladies Literary Club. The ladies had been around for more than 100 years. Membership had been dwindling over the last few decades with many of the remaining members well into their 80s. Recruiting new and younger members was not in the cards. While they owned the club house, they no longer could afford the property tax, utilities and maintenance. They decided to gift the building to an organization that would be able to take care of it while still allowing them to hold their monthly meetings in the space.

As we worked to come up with a plan to transition the building, I got to know the ladies and the history of their club. These women were inspiring! The building itself was a testament to their spirit.

In 1913, the ladies funded the construction of the building with their own money (not the money of their husbands). They paid for the lot with the proceeds from the sale of their first club house and issued bonds to raise the $25,000 needed for the construction. The total cost of the building was $32,507.94. Most of the bonds were held by the women members of the club, which was pretty much unheard of in that time. Despite the cultural beliefs and barriers, the ladies of the literary club broke through every money taboo possible.

Just to put things in perspective, this was 1913. It wasn't until 1920 that women got the right to vote, and 1974 when the Equal Credit Opportunity Act passed in the United States. Until this point, banks required all women (singled, married, widowed or divorced) to have a man co-sign any credit application, regardless of their income. Banks would also discount the wages a woman earned by as much as 50 percent when considering how much credit a woman could afford.

These ladies were movers and shakers and I loved being in their energy. The walls of the building held so much empowerment. Their story was one of breaking the mold, fighting for what was fair and equal, and supporting their community while they were at it.

Epic Failures in Negotiation–Take 2

The plan was to mirror the successful business model of the existing event center that I ran and, after renovating the building, rent the Ladies Literary Club for events.

When the news hit that we had been selected to receive the building as a gift, my boss asked if I wanted the job of managing both buildings. At the time neither of us had any idea of what that would really look like, but I said yes, as long as I was compensated. We both agreed to table the compensation conversation until we had a better idea of the workload and job description.

Over the next year I developed a business plan, operating budget, and sat on a committee to develop the renovation plan. This also meant we'd need a fundraising plan, which I just so happened to have expertise in creating. We came up with a marketing plan and new logo and cleaned out every crevice of the building (which had a huge basement *full* of over 100 years' worth of party supplies, records, and mis-matched china and fine silver to serve hundreds). We gave the building all the TLC it had not had in decades. Although the full renovation plan was going to take some time to fund, we did some minor renovations after the building was clean-ed out and began selling events.

At the same, I was also working on a proposal with the city to renew our lease at the existing event center. It had been 20 years since the city and the nonprofit had entered the lease agreement. The city decided they needed to open up the bidding process. This was a huge amount of work and uncertainty.

While the Ladies Literary Club building started out small, it soon turned into an enormous project with many moving pieces and responsibility. It also had the potential to be a great revenue source for the organization.

My busy workload had doubled. I was now running two buildings and working EVEN HARDER than ever.

We had brought the building back to life. Decades of dust and memories had been cleared for the building's renais-sance. Gone were the yellowed lace curtains, oversized 8-track media console, and frumpy mauve velvet couches. Renovation was underway to restore the drawing room back to its original state using historical photos as our guide including stripping paint and removing the false fireplace mantle to expose the original brick. We had big plans to tear out the ugly periwinkle blue carpet that flowed up the staircase, remove the dark hand-painted wallpaper, and refurbish the hardwood floors. We even had architectural renderings created to restore the grand entrance to its original 1913 glory. The building was going to be spectacular when it was finished.

And so, it was time to work out my pay structure. I carefully crafted a proposal outlining everything that had been accomplished to that point and where we were going. The operations budget for the Ladies Literary Club mirrored what was in place at the existing event center, which also meant there was a salary that mirrored mine in the budget.

I was being paid a flat salary of $40,900, and commission on the events I sold. I proposed increasing my salary to $50,000 and keeping my commission structure the same—which would essentially save the organization almost $30,000 a year. Although I really had started working in this new capacity six months prior, I did not ask for any back pay.

I wholeheartedly supported the organization and understood the need to keep our costs low while we built the business. I was willing to sacrifice a large chunk of my potential salary to see more money go into renovating the building.

Asking for a $9,100 raise pushed my comfort limit. Asking for more felt greedy and excessive, especially for a nonprofit. Several months before, my boss and I had talked about a salary increase in the range of $10,000 to $15,000. I really felt I had to keep it at the lower end—mostly out of guilt and duty to the organization. I was putting the organization's needs before my own and on the surface it somehow felt noble.

I gave my boss my proposal in early July, right before I left for a much-needed vacation. I didn't think much about it since we had already discussed most of the details. But as I unwound from the months and months of stress and thought about the details of the proposal, it hit me—this raise was *not negotiable*. I came back from vacation the next week refreshed, ready to work, and move forward.

I didn't hear a word.

I had a second vacation planned a few weeks later—July was typically the slowest time of the year and I had to plan my limited vacations around the schedule of the buildings. I left thinking surely, I would have a response back from him by the time I returned. After all, it had almost been a month.

My first day back we had our weekly meeting with our committee to strategize about the club house over lunch. After the meeting concluded, the other two committee members stopped to say hello to a few people they knew, and I took the opportunity to ask my boss if he had a chance to look at my proposal.

"I don't have an answer."

The words hit me like a brick.

"What do you mean you don't have an answer?" It had been a month! What I had proposed was more than fair. It should be a simple "*Sure, of course*" based on previous conversations.

I started to shake, and he repeated, "I don't have an answer."

"Is it because we don't know about the lease with the city?" I asked.

"Partially—there are just too many uncertainties. I just can't do it."

I was furious. Our few minutes of private discussion time were up and the conversation ended.

Later that day I received an offer—a four percent raise. Are you kidding me? A standard cost of living raise? He wanted me to double my workload for $1,636? A meager $30 a week?

We went back and forth over the next couple of weeks with several more failed and insulting meetings and emails. He told me that the Ladies Literary Club was not for personal gain and that everyone should be working on it without compensation for the betterment of the organization. He told me I had to do whatever he asked without compensation because he was the boss, otherwise I was being insubordinate.

I had put my heart and soul into the organization and what I had proposed was going to save the organization thousands in the long run.

Here I was again, knowing I had worked SO HARD, putting my employer's needs above my own, and feeling like they had bullied and taken advantage of me.

It was time to stand my ground and draw the line in the sand.

After a few agonizing and sleepless nights, I told him I was no longer willing to work on the Ladies Literary Club without being compensated as promised. I was happy to help transition this project over to another staff member, but I was not willing to work for free. I would go back to running just the one building.

That Friday afternoon, he showed up in my office and asked me to make some phone calls to potential donors for an upcoming fundraiser at the Ladies Literary Club.

"I thought I had made it pretty clear that I would not be doing anything for the Ladies Literary Club," I replied.

He didn't say a word. He turned on his heel and walked out of my office.

That weekend I worked a wedding and was at the building until 11:00 pm on Saturday night. Within a few minutes of arriving to work on Monday, I was greeted with a very stern look on my boss's face.

"I am terminating your employment here."

Money Breakthrough Questions

Where have you fallen victim to the money taboo?

Do you feel fear, guilt, or shame when you talk about money—especially if it is *your* money you are talking about?

What cultural money taboos do you hold onto? What cultural taboos have you broken free of?

What would be different in your life if you didn't apologize for what you wanted or what you have?

Where have you been holding back from earning, having, spending or stepping into being abundant or wealthy out of fear, guilt and/or shame? Is there a belief system you need to release?

Part Two
Creating a Life of Abundance

Chapter Four

Breaking Out of the Matrix

But I Worked So Hard—Doesn't That Mean Anything?

So there I was—sitting at my desk in shock from what just happened. I can't say that I was surprised, but my ego was certainly bruised.

How dare he! Doesn't he know how much I've invested into this job? It's my life! I've built the success of this place out of my sweat and tears. Hours upon hours above and beyond each week. Nights, weekends, always going the extra mile to make sure everything was perfect. I WORKED SO HARD! Why doesn't he see this? Why doesn't he appreciate this? Doesn't he give a shit how HARD I worked?

I was so furious I was shaking. I knew there was money in the budget to afford what I was asking for—I had created the budget myself. So how was it that I no longer had a job?

His excuse of not being able to afford it is complete bullshit.

It's his ego! He can't stand the idea of a woman having the potential to earn more than he does!

I was more than fair in my proposal—giving even more than I should have!

I should sue! I never had a bad review—everyone always raved about my performance. So unethical!

To make things worse, he waited until the last day of the month to fire me, which meant that my health insurance also ended that day without warning.

Over the next several weeks (and months), my brain worked overtime trying to make sense of it all and how unfair it was.

What I didn't know then that I know now is that I had a lifetime of conditioning telling me that to earn money you have to work REALLY HARD. And I had worked REALLY HARD. And now, here I was without a job—because I had worked REALLY HARD.

I hastily packed up a few personal items I had around my desk as he scornfully watched my every move. I put my keys on the table in my office and walked out the door. As I left the building, I called my husband to tell him what had happened. My voice quivered with anger and rage and then the tears began to flow.

No sooner had I hung up with my husband when my close friend Kristina called. "Mark my words—this will be the best thing that ever happened to you," she said as I wept in the front seat of my car. "Cry today, but tomorrow, move on. This is the start of something pretty amazing for you." I will never forget what she said to me that day.

I knew she was right. I knew it was time for a change. The Universe had just opened a door and pushed me through it.

The saving grace as far as my finances were concerned was that I had quite a bit of unused vacation that was paid out in my final check, along with the commission for contracts that had been signed. I had enough money in this check to buy me three months. Three months to get my shit together.

It took me less than a week to decide to open my own business. I didn't know how, I didn't have the perfect plan, but I knew it was time to stop relying on everyone else to make money.

When I talk to people who are "nine-to-fivers" about starting a business, their first response is usually one of these: "Wow! That was brave!" or "Weren't you scared?" or "What about health insurance?"

The truth of the matter is your nine-to-five job is not secure either. Not at all.

Let's talk security for a minute. I currently have 50 or 60 clients at any given time. If one of them decided she no longer wanted to work with me, while it would be disappointing, her decision certainly does not make or break my ability to make money and provide for myself. But if my boss doesn't want to work with me anymore, I'm screwed. As an entrepreneur, I am in control of my own destiny and have more security.

The Question That Shattered the Matrix

In all of the chaos that became my life that day, something pretty amazing happened. Instead of thinking "I need to find a job," I started to ask myself this question: "**What should I do?**"

Talk about S P A C E ! Being fired gave me the gift of questions. I no longer was in a panic trying to fill a void of a job; I technically just needed to fill a financial gap. I suddenly realized that filling the gap didn't need to come in the form of a new job. There was a whole new world of possibilities out there.

The question "What should I do" grew into many more questions over the next month.

Questions like:
- What skill sets do I have?
- What do I love to do?
- If I could spend my day doing anything and get paid for doing it, what would I choose?
- What does an ideal day look like for me?
- What would I like to be paid?

This newfound curiosity was the pathway to a whole new life as an entrepreneur. I cannot stress this enough. In order for me to open myself up for abundance and success, I started asking questions and not taking *anything* at face value. I allowed the Universe to speak to me and gave myself permission to do what felt right—not just do what I was told or do what I was "supposed" to do. **I broke out of the Matrix.**

For those of you who have not seen the movie *The Matrix* with Keanu Reeves, there is a moment where Keanu's character, Neo, realizes that the reality he has been living is not actually reality. It is a made-up world used to control and manipulate his thoughts and feelings and keep him plugged into the Matrix for the good of this machine that is controlling him. After unplugging, Neo learns to bend time and space because he is no longer bound by the rules of the Matrix. He is able to see his true reality and not the façade that he has been living his entire life. (For my sci-fi geeks, please forgive the very elementary description—I'm just using the image as an example.)

I think corporate culture and the pay structure that comes with it is a lot like the Matrix. We are taught (or not taught) about needing money and working hard and being subservient to companies and bosses. We are plugged into their corporate machines to produce an outcome with little or no regard for us as humans. We work because we need money, but there is often little or no joy in the workplace. We are promised bonuses, or promotions that often never come. The average American works way more than 40 hours a week, and lives for the weekend. The weekend comes and we are still attached to our phones and laptops, "trying to get caught up," answering "just a few emails," or "finishing up a project." Sunday evening comes around and we get depressed just thinking about having to go back to work the next morning. We work on vacation, we miss our kids' dance recitals and baseball games because "something came up at the office," and fall into bed exhausted at the end of each day. At some point a few people will say *enough is enough*, but they feel trapped because they need the paycheck, the medical insurance the company offers, and the "security." And so the cycle continues.

Sorry to be so depressing, but this is the reality for so many people in America and in much of the world. This was certainly most of my reality for the first 17 years of my working life. I was trapped believing the only way to get ahead was to work REALLY HARD and *hope* that one day I would get that bonus or raise or promotion that was promised to me. I gave 110 percent of everything I had to the company I was working for, expecting them to give me 110 percent back, and almost every time, I was disappointed.

If you are lucky, you might work for a company that truly values your skills and expertise and treats you well. But more often, companies leave employees feeling used and abused. So many of us enter the workforce thinking we are going to make a difference. We enter with a dream of what our lives are going to look like. Sadly, the Matrix wears us down...
...every time our brilliant idea isn't considered.
...every time our hard work isn't acknowledged.
...every time "going the extra mile" is considered the "norm" and expected.
...every time our job description grows with little or no monetary compensation.

The Matrix puts limits on how much we can make, what we can become, and what roles we can play in the companies we work for. It defines our value. It rules us with fear and scarcity. It begins to mold us into part of the corporate machine.

While this may seem overly dramatic, if you've ever worked in corporate America, I'm sure that you know what I'm talking about. And believe me, there are plenty of entre-preneurs who are also living in the Matrix. It's not just people in the corporate world who suffer from this phenomenon.

The first step to changing this is to acknowledge where you might be living in the Matrix. Where do you want to break free? Think outside of the box. Where are you existing on autopilot? Let yourself break through the boundaries that are confining you. What do you want to create? What do you want your reality to look like?

I promise you, you are stronger and more powerful than you think. And much of this power comes from being aware of where you're confined and reclaiming the passion you once had. You can love what you do *and* have money. It doesn't have to be one or the other.

The Importance of Loving What You Do

In my "glamourous" job as an event planner for an incentive travel company, we planned incentive trips for our clients' top performers. One of my biggest clients was Stampin' Up!, a multi-level marketing company that sells rubber craft stamps. While I certainly was not into stamping (I pretty much repelled all things crafty after painting those thou-sands of rolling pins), I found myself completely inspired by Shelli Gardner, the founder of Stampin' Up!, and her busi-ness model.

She was the first business owner I had seen who led with her heart. The results were undeniable. She led her company with the simple philosophy and motto of "Love What You Do." Stampin' Up! was wildly successful and growing by leaps and bounds at the time. Her message inspired her employees and the demonstrators (the people who sold her product) to build the company into a worldwide brand very quickly.

I had the honor of getting to know Shelli and the demonstrators as I planned their incentive trips. Each year they would do two trips. One was a large cruise for any demonstrator who sold a certain dollar amount, and another was a small trip for around 80 women to tour the factory in Kanab, Utah. On this trip, winners were able to spend some much-coveted, one-on-one time with Shelli.

Although their corporate offices were in Salt Lake City, Shelli kept the factory in her hometown of Kanab, nearly 300 miles away, because she was the largest employer in the small town. Manufactured products were trucked up to Salt Lake several times a week to the distribution center. Although it would have saved the company lots of money to move their manufacturing facility to Salt Lake City, Shelli recognized how important it was to have loyal employees and to be a loyal employer. For her, it felt good to keep much of the town of Kanab employed rather than making decisions only based on the bottom line.

I loved watching the women who earned these trips light up when they were around Shelli. You could see them hanging on her every word as she told the story of how she and her sister started their company. Shelli was genuine and made heart-based decisions in everything she did. She was such a great role model for women entrepreneurs.

Stampin' Up! provided a platform for many stay-at-home moms and other women who wouldn't or couldn't have a traditional job earning money. Women were empowered to earn money while doing something they loved. She created a structure that allowed women to live their current lives as homemakers, moms and wives *and* be entrepreneurs. Instead of telling them they had to fit into a mold, she inspired them to break it.

Shelli's take on business was refreshing. She cared for and nurtured employees and demonstrators who were like family. In return, they supported and loved Shelli and the company.

Stampin' Up! was a stark juxtaposition to where I was working—a company that stopped paying overtime and bonuses and took advantage of their employees to make a buck. I had learned to accept this greed as "normal" corporate behavior. When I saw the two companies side by side, I seriously felt like I had sold my soul to the devil. I now could see there was a better, kinder, more respectful way.

Inspired, I knew I wanted to create a life for myself where I loved what I did. I didn't know how this was going to happen, but I knew that loving what I did was now a top priority in choosing where and how I worked. I knew I needed to break free. It was my first glimpse that I was plugged into the Matrix.

Part of this realization came when my good friend sent me a copy of Steve Job's Stanford graduation speech. I was feeling burned out, defeated, and miserable working SO HARD and not being compensated or recognized for all the time and energy I was expending. (Do I sound like a broken record here? Hello, money sabotage patterns!) I was contemplating leaving my job for greener pastures and dreamed about what it would be like to "love what you do."

The speech is seriously one of the most inspiring things I have ever read, and so much of it rang true at the time, and still does today. It's long—but I've included the entire speech because it is *that* good. I read it every time I need a reminder of what is really important in life. Note: emphasis mine.

I am honored to be with you today at your commencement from one of the finest universities in the world. I never graduated from college. Truth be told, this is the closest I've ever gotten to a college graduation. Today I want to tell you three stories from my life. That's it. No big deal. Just three stories.

The first story is about connecting the dots.

I dropped out of Reed College after the first six months, but then stayed around as a drop-in for another 18 months or so before I really quit. So why did I drop out?

It started before I was born. My biological mother was a young, unwed college graduate student, and she decided to put me up for adoption. She felt very strongly that I should be adopted by college graduates, so everything was all set for me to be adopted at birth by a lawyer and his wife. Except that when I popped out they decided at the last minute that they really wanted a girl. So my parents, who were on a waiting list, got a call in the middle of the night asking: "We have an unexpected baby boy; do you want him?" They said: "Of course." My biological mother later found out that my mother had never graduated from college and that my father had never graduated from high school. She refused to sign the final adoption papers. She only relented a few months later when my parents promised that I would someday go to college.

Seventeen years later I did go to college. But I naively chose a college that was almost as expensive as Stanford, and all of my working-class parents' savings were being spent on my college tuition. After six months, I couldn't see the value in it. I had no idea what I wanted to do with my life and no idea how college was going to help me figure it out. And here I was spending all of the money my parents had saved their entire life. So I decided to drop out and trust that it would all work out OK.

It was pretty scary at the time, but looking back it was one of the best decisions I ever made. The minute I dropped out I could stop taking the required classes that didn't interest me, and begin dropping in on the ones that looked interesting.

It wasn't all romantic. I didn't have a dorm room, so I slept on the floor in friends' rooms, I returned Coke bottles for the 5¢ deposits to buy food with, and I would walk the seven miles across town every Sunday night to get one good meal a week at the Hare Krishna temple. I loved it. **And much of what I**

stumbled into by following my curiosity and intuition turned out to be priceless later on. Let me give you one example:

Reed College at that time offered perhaps the best calligraphy instruction in the country. Throughout the campus every poster, every label on every drawer, was beautifully hand calligraphed. Because I had dropped out and didn't have to take the normal classes, I decided to take a calligraphy class to learn how to do this. I learned about serif and san serif typefaces, about varying the amount of space between different letter combinations, about what makes great typography great. It was beautiful, historical, artistically subtle in a way that science can't capture, and I found it fascinating.

None of this had even a hope of any practical application in my life. But 10 years later, when we were designing the first Macintosh computer, it all came back to me. And we designed it all into the Mac. It was the first computer with beautiful typography. If I had never dropped in on that single course in college, the Mac would have never had multiple typefaces or proportionally spaced fonts.

And since Windows just copied the Mac, it's likely that no personal computer would have them. If I had never dropped out, I would have never dropped in on this calligraphy class, and personal computers might not have the wonderful typography that they do. **Of course, it was impossible to connect the dots looking forward when I was in college. But it was very, very clear looking backwards 10 years later.**

Again, you can't connect the dots looking forward; you can only connect them looking backwards. So **you have to trust that the dots will somehow connect in your future.** You have to trust in something—your gut, destiny, life, karma, whatever. This approach has never let me down, and it has made all the difference in my life.

My second story is about love and loss.

I was lucky—I found what I loved to do early in life. Woz and I started Apple in my parents' garage when I was 20. We worked hard, and in 10 years Apple had grown from just the two of us in a garage into a $2 billion company with over 4,000 employees. We had just released our finest creation—the Macintosh—a year earlier, and I had just turned 30. And then I got fired. How can *you get fired from a company you started? Well, as Apple grew we hired someone who I thought was very talented to run the company with me, and for the first year or so things went well. But then our visions of the future began to diverge and eventually we had a falling out. When we did, our Board of Directors sided with him. So at 30 I was out. And very publicly out. What had been the focus of my entire adult life was gone, and it was devastating.*

I really didn't know what to do for a few months. I felt that I had let the previous generation of entrepreneurs down—that I had dropped the baton as it was being passed to me. I met with David Packard and Bob Noyce and tried to apologize for screwing up so badly. I was a very public failure, and I even thought about running away from the valley. But something slowly began to dawn on me—I still loved what I did. The turn of events at Apple had not changed that one bit. **I had been rejected, but I was still in love. And so I decided to start over.**

I didn't see it then, but it turned out that **getting fired from Apple was the best thing that could have ever happened to me.** *The heaviness of being successful was replaced by the lightness of being a beginner again, less sure about everything. It freed me to enter one of the most creative periods of my life.*

During the next five years, I started a company named NeXT, another company named Pixar, and fell in love with an amazing woman who would become my wife. Pixar went on to create the world's first computer animated feature film, Toy Story, and is now the most successful animation studio in the world. In a remarkable turn of events, Apple bought NeXT, I returned to Apple, and the technology we developed at NeXT is at the heart of Apple's current renaissance. And Laurene and I have a wonderful family together.

I'm pretty sure none of this would have happened if I hadn't been fired from Apple. It was awful tasting medicine, but I guess the patient needed it. Sometimes life hits you in the head with a brick. Don't lose faith. **I'm convinced that the only thing that kept me going was that I loved what I did. You've got to find what you love.** *And that is as true for your work as it is for your lovers. Your work is going to fill a large part of your life, and the only way to be truly satisfied is to do what you believe is great work. And the only way to do great work is to love what you do. If you haven't found it yet, keep looking. Don't settle. As with all matters of the heart, you'll know when you find it. And, like any* *great relationship, it just gets better and better as the years roll on. So keep looking until you find it. Don't settle.*

My third story is about death.

When I was 17, I read a quote that went something like: "If you live each day as if it was your last, someday you'll most certainly be right." It made an impression on me, and since then, for the past 33 years, I have looked in the mirror every morning and asked myself: **"If today were the last day of my life, would I want to do what I am about to do today?" And whenever the answer has been "No" for too many days in a row, I know I need to change something.**

Remembering that I'll be dead soon is the most important tool I've ever encountered to help me make the big choices in life. Because almost everything—all external expectations, all pride, all fear of embarrassment or failure—these things just fall away in the face of death, leaving only what is truly important. Remembering that you are going to die is the best way I know to avoid the trap of thinking you have something to lose. You are already naked. There is no reason not to follow your heart.

About a year ago I was diagnosed with cancer. I had a scan at 7:30 in the morning, and it clearly showed a tumor on my pancreas. I didn't even know what a pancreas was. The doctors told me this was almost certainly a type of cancer that is incurable, and that I should expect to live no longer than three to six months. My doctor advised me to go home and get my affairs in order, which is doctor's code for prepare to die.

It means to try to tell your kids everything you thought you'd have the next 10 years to tell them in just a few months. It means to make sure everything is buttoned up so that it will be as easy as possible for your family. It means to say your goodbyes.

I lived with that diagnosis all day. Later that evening I had a biopsy, where they stuck an endoscope down my throat, through my stomach and into my intestines, put a needle into my pancreas and got a few cells from the tumor. I was sedated, but my wife, who was there, told me that when they viewed the cells under a microscope the doctors started crying because it turned out to be a very rare form of pancreatic cancer that is curable with surgery. I had the surgery and I'm fine now.

This was the closest I've been to facing death, and I hope it's the closest I get for a few more decades. Having lived through it, I can now say this to you with a bit more certainty than when death was a useful but purely intellectual concept:

*No one wants to die. Even people who want to go to heaven don't want to die to get there. And yet death is the destination we all share. No one has ever escaped it. And that is as it should be, because Death is very likely the single best invention of Life. It is Life's change agent. It clears out the old to make way for the new. Right now, the new is you, but someday not too long from now, you will gradually become the old and be cleared away. Sorry to be so dramatic, but it is quite true. **Your time is limited, so don't waste it living someone else's life. Don't be trapped by dogma—which is living with the results of other people's thinking.** Don't let the noise of other's opinions drown out your own inner voice. And most important, have the courage to follow your heart and intuition. They somehow already know what you truly want to become. Everything else is secondary.*

When I was young, there was an amazing publication called The Whole Earth Catalog, which was one of the bibles of my generation. It was created by a fellow named Stewart Brand not far from here in Menlo Park, and he brought it to life with his poetic touch. This was in the late 1960s, before personal computers and desktop publishing, so it was all made with typewriters, scissors, and Polaroid cameras. It was sort of like Google in paperback form, 35 years before Google came along: it was idealistic and overflowing with neat tools and great notions.

Stewart and his team put out several issues of The Whole Earth Catalog, and then when it had run its course, they put out a final issue. It was the mid-1970s, and I was your age. On the back cover of their final issue was a photograph of an early morning country road, the kind you might find yourself hitchhiking on if you were so adventurous. Beneath it were the words: "Stay Hungry. Stay Foolish." It was their farewell message as they signed off. Stay Hungry. Stay Foolish. And I have always wished that for myself. And now, as you graduate to begin anew, I wish that for you.

Stay Hungry. Stay Foolish.

Thank you all very much.
—Steve Jobs, Stanford University, June 14, 2005

Steve Jobs and I have a lot in common. I, too, had gone to Reed College, and I dropped out of Reed for many of the same reasons. Ironically, several years after reading this for the first time, I also got fired from a job I loved and felt like I'd lost everything. And I had much the same renaissance in building from the ashes and starting my own business. I have also learned that trusting my intuition is crucial—and the dots you follow don't always show you where you're going. But when you look back, it all makes sense.

But beyond the similarities in our life stories, this is what I take away—no matter where you are in your money journey, nothing is more important, as Jobs reminds, than loving what you do. Nothing. Abundance doesn't come from working REALLY HARD at a job you hate or heeding other's opinions about what you should be doing or not doing.

How to Live Outside the Matrix

I think it is safe to say I now live outside the Matrix. From this vantage point, I would like to offer a bit of advice and reflection for those of you who are still trying to break free.

Working hard doesn't really get you where you think it will—especially working for someone who doesn't appreciate you. It is critical to love your job and not feel victim to the grind.

Set your own boundaries. Make sure you are conscious about how much you are giving to your work in exchange for what you are receiving. This is true not only if you are working for someone else, but also if you are working for yourself. Don't let your clients turn into your old boss (I will explore this more in the coming chapters).

Gratitude is everything. Every day I am grateful for the clients I work with. I love our relationship. I love that I get to help them build businesses. I love that I can help them understand their numbers in a way that makes sense to them. I love that I am able to do what I love on my own terms. I make my own schedule, work from home, and take off a random Tuesday when I have friends in town to hang out at the beach. I try to incorporate #funfridays where I do something really fun on a Friday just because I can, or #memondays where I do something to nourish my soul. I am grateful I am doing something I am passionate about.

Be deliberate. The life I now live is a result of very deliberate decisions. Every day I make a choice to focus on doing things I love and things that bring me joy. I have created a life that allows me to have control over what I do and when I do it. I have chosen a life that gives me SPACE. Just like Steve Jobs, if there are too many days in a row where I don't like what I am doing, I know something needs to change.

> *"I'm trying to free your mind.*
> *But I can only show you the door.*
> *You're the one who has to walk through it."*
> *—Morpheus, The Matrix*

Money Breakthrough Questions

What do you want to do? Don't worry about if you think it's possible or start making excuses about why it won't work. What do you love to do? What would your ideal day look like? What would you like to be paid for doing and how much would you like to be paid for doing that thing? How would you like to spend your time?

Think about where you might be caught in the Matrix: Are there people, employers, clients, situations that are controlling you and keeping you from living the way you want to live your life? What boundaries are confining you? What do you want to create? What do you want your reality to look like?

Where have you broken out of the Matrix?

Make a list of what you love to do. This isn't just work-related. Seriously, make a list of *everything* that brings you joy. Write an action plan of how you want to incorporate more of these things into your life. If the list feels overwhelming, start with a teeny tiny step that will send you in the right direction.

What are you grateful for in your life?

Who inspires you to live your best life? What about their story inspires you?

Chapter Five

The Cost of Doing Business

About 10 years before I was fired, I explored the idea of opening my own event planning business. I did a bunch of research, and even came up with a name and a logo design. And then I chickened out. While I was great at planning, I was scared to follow through.

Fast forward to the day I drove away from my office in tears with a box of personal items and no plan. Suddenly jobless, I needed to figure out a way to make money—and fast. This put me in a state of desperation, which often is where people energetically make decisions about earning and spending money.

I spent a few weeks researching job openings, perfecting my resumé, filing for unemployment, and exploring taking legal action against my boss for firing me.

One thing I was very aware of, within the first few days of being fired, was the negative energy that surrounded me when I came from a place of desperation, anger and resentment. As much as I wanted revenge for the "wrong" that had been done, it was crystal clear that my energy was much better spent focusing on my future rather than my past.

While I was eligible to take unemployment, I felt guilty

"living off the system." By the time the waiting period was over, I knew I would be starting my own business, and the thought of applying for jobs I would never accept felt so heavy. So, I let the idea of an unemployment check go. I knew that, somehow, the money would come.

Desperation Pricing

As I was researching how to price services for a consulting business, I read somewhere that you should charge three times what you would be paid if you were employed by the company.

Three times! You have got to be kidding. No way will people pay that! I am not worth that much money!

Looking back, I wish I would have believed what I read. So many entrepreneurs—especially women—undervalue their services. We are so concerned with what people are going to think. We think we are incapable of delivering the perceived value. I like to call this desperation pricing, and it sounds a little like this:

- No one will pay this—what if I don't have any clients?
- What if they don't like the service or product I provide?
- What if they think I am a fraud?
- What will they think of me?
- They will think I am greedy for asking for such a high rate.
- I am setting myself up for failure.
- I should look at what others are charging and make sure my prices are less since I don't have _____ (fill in the blank: *experience, credentials, client base,* etc.)
- I love what I do and just want to help people—I don't need to be paid.
- I don't need that much.

The truth of the matter is most female entrepreneurs coming out of the Matrix suffer from over-delivering and under-charging. While so much of this is a direct result of your money mindset, it ultimately comes back to what you perceive as your value and worth (or what you have been conditioned to believe is your value and worth by the Matrix), *and* your ability to receive what others want to give you in return for your services.

Desperation pricing often comes from a place of scarcity, not abundance. If you are scared you won't have any clients, you price yourself low to ensure your sales come rolling in. But this is a catch-22. You might get the clients, but can you then deliver your product and make money for the low price you have promised, and is it sustainable?

The problem with approaching your business pricing just to fill a gap is that usually you are only seeing a tiny little piece of what is possible. Often when a business is built on a fill-the-gap pricing model, it has been set up to fail.

A sustainable business model is not something most entre-preneurs think about when they are first starting up. There is a huge rush to go out and sell and get the clients, but very little thought is given to how you are going to handle the work that comes in. For instance, what happens when you price yourself so low in order to attract clients that you get 10 new clients in one day? Will you have the time and energetic resources to deliver what you sell?

In the first few weeks of getting fired, I received an offer from a couple of friends for $20 an hour to help them build their business. It was my first true consulting job, and significantly less than I wanted to be making. But since I had no job, it seemed like a good place to start. It also helped me stretch my last paycheck a bit further and gave me more time to figure out a game plan for my business.

Over the next few months I did some serious soul-searching

and really focused on what exactly it was that I loved to do. I took an inventory of my skill sets and imagined how I could sell them. My superpowers are organization and project management and I came up with a list with every single place I could use them and make money. The list included event planning, financial services and personal assistant services. Although all of these normally would not go together in a business model, I wanted to make sure I left no opportunity to make money on the table. And that is how **All the Details Consulting** was born.

My initial rate was $35 an hour, regardless of the service. In my mind, this was a "fair" price, much more than I had been making, and it felt right. With this pricing, I would easily be able to fill my financial gap and have a little bit of time to grow my business. I had a logo designed, put up a very simple DYI website and printed some business cards. I was off like a rocket.

Recreating the Matrix—How I Ended Up with More Clients Than I Could Handle

Thanks to a women's networking group I belonged to, I already had some great connections. Within a few months, I was onboarding at least one new client a week and felt elated with my success at finding potential clients and closing the deal on a regular basis.

My 10-second pitch, "I help you get your shit together," worked like a charm. Other than printing my business cards I had almost no advertising expenses. Clients were coming at me from every direction and it felt fantastic!

A growth plan never crossed my mind. I never considered what would happen if I kept this pace up, never thought about where I would be a couple of years down the road. I was just happy making more than I ever had before. I was filling the gap and then some. This felt like amazing success.

I said yes to everything. I did medical billing, inbox sorting and office systematizing—anything that needed organizational skills to complete. I even took a class in how to do tax preparation and thought I would file people's returns.

On my first website I listed out every type of event and event-related task I could handle for clients. I listed financial services including payroll, budgeting, and financial organization. I listed personal assistance and special projects that included nonprofit board retreats, fundraising plans, general organization, email and address book management. I even listed itinerary planning for travel or out-of-town guests.

Anything you need done, I can make sure it happens! was my tag line at the bottom of the page.

Even my business card highlighted four very different things: event planning, bookkeeping, tax preparation, personal assistance. My rates were low, and I was willing to do just about anything within my skill set that would make me money.

I am not super proud of this, but it got me clients.

A *lot* of clients.

The Lack of a Plan

All of this "success" came from a place of fear, desperation, and scarcity. I was terrified I was not going to fill the gap and pay my bills. Instead of approaching my business with a solid plan, my only goal was to get clients, make money to fill the gap, and figure it out as I go.

It's not that I did anything wrong. Lots of people do it this way and there is something to be said about having the guts to do it.

I honestly had no idea what a huge need there was for bookkeeping. I thought that events would be the mainstay of my business and bookkeeping would be my side gig. But just about everyone I spoke with needed help with their money.

I threw myself into business with the need to make money, and fast—I had no entrance plan and no business plan. Looking back, thank God I didn't, because I'm not sure I would have had the momentum or courage to keep going forward if I'd spent that time planning. However, in order for me to be sustainable and succeed long-term, I had to be open to evaluating and shifting things, so I didn't burn out.

I didn't do it this way, but now I know that if you take the time to really position yourself for growth sooner rather than later, you set yourself up for long-term success. Not just in your business, but in the quality of your life.

This way, you are able to enjoy your work *and* have time for yourself. Isn't having time and freedom to do what you want one of the main reasons you went into business for yourself anyway? So why do so many entrepreneurs fall into the trap of working even harder on and in their business than they did in the corporate world?

Think of planning like a map—you want to know where you are going before you head out on that long road trip. You want an entrance plan, an exit plan, a self-care plan, and a how-to-stay-above-water plan.

Have I ever seen a business with all of these plans in place? No. But that doesn't mean that you shouldn't think about it or that it's too late to start.

A Victim of Time

About a year into my business, I started to notice I was running out of time. I was trading hours for dollars, and while I had plenty of dollars in my pocket, my time was becoming more and more limited.

I was working 10-plus hour days during the week and at least five or six hours on Saturdays and Sundays. I was making more money than I ever had before, but I had no time to enjoy it. I would get up at 5:00 am (I am an early bird) and start working immediately. I wouldn't look up from my laptop until I needed to jump in the shower and rush out the door for client appointments. While I loved morning hikes in the hills behind my house, I rarely got out because my clients' needs always came first. At the end of the day I would spend an hour or two responding to emails and allocating my hours into a time-tracking app so I could invoice my clients at the end of the month.

Every time a new client approached me, I said yes. Who doesn't want to say yes to more money, right? But I desperately wanted to say no because I couldn't possibly fit another client into my week. I eventually stopped networking because I couldn't take on the clients that would flock to me every time I showed up.

I knew something needed to change. What kind of business owner feels panic when someone wants to work with them? I saw two ways I could grow: increase my prices and have fewer clients *or* hire someone to help do the work so I could take on more clients. Neither one of these really excited me or felt right.

The idea of having fewer clients and making more felt like the easiest solution, but there wasn't a single client I wanted to "fire," so I decided to increase my prices. I hoped a few clients would self-select and decide to leave. But there was one problem with this plan. No one left. Not one single client. And even with the higher rates (which really weren't that much higher in retrospect), I still attracted new clients.

Shortly after my rate increase, I hired someone to help me with data entry. That is not the bulk of my workload. While it eased the load a little, it wasn't enough. What I needed was someone who could work directly with my clients. Like so many entrepreneurs do, I needed a mini-me.

I put out a job description and received some pretty decent resumés. I selected the best candidate and gave her a book-keeping project as a trial. It was a disaster. But it wasn't her fault—it boiled down to the fact that I wasn't ready to give up control. I felt no one could do it like me. My clients hired me for *me*, not my company. No one would work as hard as I could. Bottom line: I wasn't ready to delegate.

I was a "victim of time"—my pricing and my unwillingness to give up control insured that I would keep every hour of every week jam-packed....and also insured I would eventually burn out.

Lots of people suffer from being a victim of time. Not just entrepreneurs. So many of us miss out on life as we spend all of our time and energy working hard and trying to get ahead. We believe that hard work is the only way to get where we want to be. It is probably the biggest symptom of being caught in the Matrix.

When you are a victim of time, there is no space to grow. You want more than anything to have time and freedom to enjoy life, but you feel you have to spend all of your time and energy working to build your business. You repeat stories like these: "I have to do it all myself" or "I can't afford to hire it out" or "It's easier to do it myself" or, my personal favorite: "No one can do it better than I can." And then the self-sabotage surfaces. You take on too much and can't meet deadlines or you meet potential clients and don't follow up. The very things you are doing to build your business start to fail because you don't have the time to follow through.

Boundaries to Avoid Burnout

According to the Small Business Association, 30 percent of businesses fail in the first two years, 50 percent during the first five years, and 66 percent during the first 10. That means only 34 percent of businesses will celebrate their 10-year anniversary.[2]

Sure, a lot of this can be chalked up to people who don't know how to manage a business and cash flow, but I think the deeper problem is the *true* cost of doing business on many different levels. The cost of doing business also needs to include:

- The amount of time you spend working rather than enjoying life
- The stress you feel
- The impact on your family
- The amount of energy it really takes to run a business
- The toll it takes on your health
- The energy it takes to combat exhaustion and burn-out

The cost of running your own business is so much more than paying for advertising and insurance. Starting a business takes grit and perseverance, and at the end of the day you have to ask yourself—is it really worth it?

One of my favorite clients has a small framed saying hanging in their office. The first part is handwritten in red crayon, the last of the phrase is crossed out and changed and finished in blue crayon:

> *Do what you love and you'll ~~never work a day in your life~~ work super fucking hard all the time with no separation or any boundaries and also take everything extremely personally.*

The first time I saw this I literally laughed out loud. Sad, but soooooo true.

Here is the big question—**when you start a business, are**

---

[2] Smartbiz, SBA Loans Made Easy, Web, 30 September, 2019
https://resources.smartbizloans.com/blog/business-finances/percentage-of-businesses-that-fail-and-why/

you bringing the Matrix right along with you? Sadly, many times the answer to this question is yes.

So, what's the solution? **Better boundaries.**

Boundaries include:
- Valuing your expertise and time so you don't over-deliver
- Pricing yourself for profit
- Knowing your limits and skills—this means working in your zone of genius and outsourcing everything else (Read *The Big Leap* by Gay Hendricks for more on this topic!)
- Putting yourself first—taking mandatory time off to relax and enjoy your life, including time for exercise and your physical and mental health

In order to create boundaries that protect your precious time, you first have to define the **value of your time**. Keep in mind, this is so much more than the rate you charge your clients. It also figures in how you show up for yourself, your colleagues and your clients, and the amount of time you dedicate to various tasks within your business.

One of the hardest lessons I had to learn as an entrepreneur was how to find my value after having been told for years what I was worth inside the corporate Matrix. I constantly sabotaged myself by undervaluing and over-delivering and simply recreated the Matrix in my business—just replacing my boss with my clients.

Once you have your boundaries set, be sure to create systems and structures that support your boundaries. This can be blocking out time on your calendar for personal time, saying no when you need to, or outsourcing things like social media and bookkeeping.

Burnout is real. It is honestly one of the biggest costs of doing business. As much as you might resist them, remember boundaries are your friend.

Sometimes Less Is More

One of my clients has been in business for about four years. Like me, she has been extremely successful in attracting clients with her below-market-rate pricing. She is also on the verge of burnout. She works incredibly hard and is constantly dealing with employees who don't care as much about her business as she does. Always hiring and firing, she never seems to have a reliable crew to get her projects done, which in turn causes even more stress and long hours.

Our heart-to-heart talks have included ideas for her next steps. She's facing what I faced. Does she really want to grow her business by taking on more clients, and therefore more employees? Or does she want to choose her favorite clients, raise her rates and scale back?

There is this underlying mythology in our society that we should work harder and push and push and push to get more clients and more money. It's called *the hustle*, and it's a trait that's revered in the entrepreneurial world.

When I started to get more and more clients and make more money, I started to notice this feeling of longing. It wasn't that I wanted more—it was actually that I wanted less. It was the anti-hustle. I wanted fewer clients and more time. I wanted less stress so I could enjoy what little downtime I had. Earning money just to have money wasn't fulfilling to me at all. My dream was to earn money so I could have more space and time to do the things I loved, not just keep working harder. What I was creating didn't look anything like that.

In business, you hear a lot about **scaling** and **leveraging**.

When you **scale**, you take what you are doing and make it bigger. As the business owner, you hire people to take on some or most of your tasks. Scaling might look like adding more employees or increasing the quantity of products you deliver so you can grow your business, gain more clients, and reach more people. If executed well, scaling should allow you to expand and still stay profitable.

Leveraging is making a conscious decision about the best use of your time and resources in a way that brings you more income for less work. Examples of leveraging are creating passive income products, packaging your offerings, and providing services that are one to many (like group programs and events) rather than one-on-one client interactions. Leveraging allows you to stop trading hours for dollars.

Neither is right or wrong, but they certainly are different approaches. It is possible to do both, and many successful growth plans include both scaling and leveraging. Both involve working smarter, not harder. You need to make the choice that works for you. It's ok if you decide you don't want to scale and get bigger. Your business should work for you— rather than *you working for the business*. Your business should provide you with the lifestyle you want—not just financially, but in time and space and freedom.

It's never too late to evaluate where you are and where you want to be. Think of the lifestyle you're living as the return on your investment of time, energy and money in your business. It is *always* ok to make a shift if your business is not providing you the life you want.

Just because you start on one path doesn't mean you have to follow that path forever. If you aren't happy, change something. If you are feeling on the verge of burnout, make the shifts in your business that will support your well-being. It is always ok to say no to potential clients or projects that aren't a good fit. You have to decide if the cost of doing business is worth the return on investment.

Money Breakthrough Questions

Do you think you are pricing from a place of desperation? Why or why not?

What are your fears around pricing? (If you work in a nine-to-five job, replace "pricing" with "salary negotiation.")

Where are you just filling the gap vs. pricing from a place of abundance?

Where are you bringing the Matrix into your entrepreneurial life?

Do you have an exit plan? What about a self-care plan? What can you put in place to position yourself for growth in a way that is aligned with the direction you want to grow?

Do you feel like you are a victim of time? Why or why not?

What boundaries do you currently have in place? What do you do to enforce these boundaries? Are there any new boundaries you need to set up? What would that look like for you?

What are your goals for growth? Do you want to scale or leverage, or both? What does that look like for your business and how does that align with the cost of doing business?

What is the true cost (financial, emotional, physical, spiritual) of running your business?

Chapter Six

Aligning the Stars for Success

I was very close to my grandfather Bill. The most influential and unforgettable person in my life, he taught me so many things about money—including credit and why it was so important to have a good credit score. When I was in college and ready to buy my first new car (to replace the one I bought in high school with my rolling pin earnings), rather than loaning or giving me the money, he put up the money at the local credit union so I could take the loan out in my own name and start building my credit.

A few years after I was married, my husband and I built a house together with Bill. At that time my grandmother was transitioning into full-time care for dementia; she passed away a couple of years after we moved in. We designed the house to have separate living spaces, so Bill had his own kitchen, laundry room, great room, bedrooms and office in the basement, complete with his own patio and entrance from the garage.

For most of the 14 years we lived together, he was very active and traveled all over the world with his good friend Bob, who had also lost his wife. Bob would stay with us every other weekend and on the opposite weekends, Bill would stay at Bob's house. We used to joke about the two 80-year-old teenagers who lived in our basement. They had martini hour every Friday and Saturday (and sometimes during the week). Being around the two of them was really a lesson in how to live brilliantly. "Life begins at 80," Bill used to say. Watching him and Bob, I couldn't deny the truth in that statement.

As Bill entered his 90s, he began to slow down and he, too, started to show signs of dementia. Shortly after this, Bob had a fall and passed away fairly suddenly. The last 18 months of my grandfather's life were pretty hard on me— watching the man who had lived so fully fade away right before my eyes was heartbreaking.

Also, in addition to running my business, I now was handling all of his affairs including managing his in-home care and his finances and running interference between his ever-changing personality and his caretakers.

We had a set of interior French doors at the bottom of the stairwell that separated our living space from his. On December 16, 2016 at 6:00 am the French doors blew open. In the 14 years of living in the house, this had only happened once or twice before on blustery days. I have no doubt that Bob pushed those doors open to make me jump out of bed and bring me downstairs. When I walked into his bedroom to check on him, I saw Bill lying in his bed, struggling to sit up. He couldn't talk but he was desperately trying to communicate with me. Bill had suffered a stroke.

"Do you need to get up and go to the bathroom?" I asked. He nodded yes.

His caretaker was not due to arrive until 7:00 am, so I called for my husband Brian to come downstairs. We got him out of bed and into the bathroom. As we were bringing him back to bed, he collapsed. Within a few short minutes he transitioned from this world as I held his hand and said goodbye. It was beautiful, heartbreaking, and magical.

As difficult as it was to lose him, I knew he had gained his angelic superpowers on the other side and my biggest cheerleader had leveled up. Over the next several months I could feel him with me everywhere I turned. He was sending signs that he was helping me—messages on license plates, songs on the radio, the wind blowing through the wind chimes that were given to me as a gift to remind me of him.

The Need for Change

Something big was brewing. I could feel it in every fiber of my being. Too many things were showing up to ignore the signs. It was Spring 2017 and stars were aligning.

I was still grieving the loss of my grandfather and feeling the stress of closing his estate while managing my client workload. I was exhausted. While I loved what I did and I loved my clients, there was rarely a day where I wasn't scrambling to try and stay on top of an ever-growing to-do list.

As I mentioned, I was attracting more clients than I could handle. I know, I know—it's a great problem to have, but a problem, nonetheless. I had no time to enjoy the life I was creating. I was still in the same old pattern. I couldn't say no to new business, and I was afraid to let go of control and hire a team. Worry kept me up at night. What if I let my clients down? What if I hire someone and I'm not a good boss? What if I mess up what I have worked so hard to build?

It was pretty clear; burnout had arrived. It was time to change my structure from the inside out.

Awakening at Ignite

In late March of that year I was cleaning out my email inbox and opened a newsletter from a client. I always like seeing what my clients are up to, but very rarely read through all the details. Perhaps it was fate or maybe destiny. I scrolled through all of her upcoming events and happenings.

The word "Soulpreneur" caught my eye. My client's colleague was hosting a three-day event called Ignite the last week of April. The name, the brief description and the graphics really spoke to me. I knew nothing about the host or the event, but somehow, I knew I had to be there.

But *three days*? At that point, I couldn't take an afternoon off without having to stay up until midnight to get my work done. How would I ever take the time out of my busy schedule to attend three whole days of classes?

The first day of the event, I felt apprehensive. I opened the double doors and walked into the room thinking if it is horrible, I can leave and not come back.

What happened over the next three days was nothing short of magical.

Within the first couple of hours I had taken over a dozen pages of notes. While the event's main focus was on marketing, it really was about possibility and asking questions that open up space for transformation. And let me tell you, the doors and windows of possibility blew wide open.

At the end of the first day, a speaker was scheduled to talk about money. Of course, I was excited about the topic and couldn't wait to hear the discussion—especially with this group of people!

We were told to bring 10 one dollar bills. Everyone laid their money neatly on the table in front of them. The speaker chose a few volunteers and whispered some secret directions to them. Then the group of selected volunteers spread out around the room and at the same time, began gathering up everyone's dollar bills—without saying a word.

It pushed a lot of buttons.

After the room calmed down, we processed what had happened. Many of the volunteers felt horrible taking the money. Many of the people at the tables had issues with having money taken without consent, although no one stopped it from happening. The tension was thick in the room. Although it was just 10 dollars, it brought up so much emotion.

It felt chaotic and uncomfortable and I loved it. What a brilliant exercise in receiving, having and losing money.

The next morning, we continued the discussion around the money exercise. Several people got up and expressed frustration, confusion, anger. One person asked for her 10 dollars back.

In all this fear and scarcity, I knew I had to get up and talk. I could feel it in every cell of my body. My perception of money was so different from what others were saying, and I had to share it.

I walked up to the mic. I barely knew three people in the room of 80 and I was nervous to share such a personal story, but I couldn't stay quiet. I took a deep breath and told my money story. I told a whole room of strangers about getting fired and standing up for myself. I was vulnerable and real. I talked about my experience as a bookkeeper and what I had observed about people and money—what I was saying would become many of the concepts in this book. As I was telling my story, I could feel myself stepping into a space of empowerment. It felt amazing.

After I finished, Angella Johnson, the host of the event, asked the audience, "Who in this room needs a bookkeeper?" And at least 75 percent of the room raised their hand.

SHIT! I can't take on that many clients—but every single person in here is my ideal client!

Oh My God, I am screwed—I already have too many clients and no time!

I'm going to have to say no to all of them.

The old agonizing constriction kicked in. I immediately shrunk back in fear and felt defeated.

Following Intuition

Later that afternoon, I was talking with a friend during a break when I was approached by one of the attendees.

"I really felt a spark when you were talking," she said. "Here's my business card."

I said thank you and took her card. I assumed she wanted to talk about hiring me for bookkeeping. Usually in situations like this, I would smile, put the card in my purse, and never think about it again until months later when I would empty out the bottom of my purse and throw the cards I had collected into the trash. I simply didn't have the bandwidth for more clients but wanted to be polite.

The next morning, I woke up early, and rather than going straight to work on client tasks before the session started, I took some much-needed, and rather rare personal time to process everything I had soaked in the day before. My brain was overflowing. I had to journal out what I was feeling. What came out was pure inspiration and premonition.

How I want to transform bookkeeping:
I want to lead my business with magic to create magic in my clients' businesses.
I want to create a client experience that heals their relationship with money.
I want to be an advisor of financial awareness that shows my clients a new way.
I create the systems that help them manage their business in a magical way—that allows them to be magical in what they do best.
I want to Unleash the Beautiful, Magical Conscious Soul of Abundant Money.
I want to help clients stop avoiding and stressing about money so they can become abundant.
I want to be a truth guide for money.
I want to add in a component of speaking and educating and maybe even write a book.
I want to train clients on abundance and not chasing money.
I want to train on fundraising with heart.
I need to market for the right employees—ideal would be money and events but who I hire needs to be willing to be magical.
I want employees who show up for our clients.
I want employees who don't judge our clients' relationships with money.

As I was writing out this wish list and dreaming about how my life and business could transform, I had a strong urge to look up the person who handed me her business card. Priscilla Stephan, Intuitive Business Strategist. Her tagline read—*Lead From Your Soul.* There is was again: the word *Soul*.

I went to her website and was immediately drawn in as I read these words:

Most likely you love what you do, but you've reached an upper limit in your business.
You are afraid of losing yourself as you scale—and your confidence may be wavering.
You might even be lacking clarity of direction as you are called into your next evolution of leadership.
You are excited to expand your vision to new heights, but there is something holding you back from your next level of impact and business growth.

Check. Check. Check. Everything about her—the energy in her photos, her descriptions about how she helped entrepreneurs, even her mention of how she liked everything that sparkles. (So do I!) Every single word spoke to my soul.

I was crying. Was this everything I had been asking for?

Let me be honest. I did not go to Ignite looking for a business coach. Up until this point I never had thought I needed one. After all, I was successfully bringing in clients left and right. Why would I pay for a coach to help me expand this ever-growing problem? But this somehow felt different.

As soon I walked into the event space that morning, I found Priscilla.

"I went to your website and you are everything I have been looking for. I don't know what it looks like, but I need you in my life," I told her.

She squealed with excitement. After telling her about my experience that morning, we both shed a few tears. We both knew it was no accident we had been brought together.

As we were discussing the logistics of connecting, I asked her where she lived.

"San Diego," she replied.

"I *knew* it!"

When I told her I lived in Utah she immediately said, "No, you need to live somewhere with more sunshine."

I smirked. "Yes, moving to San Diego has been something I have always dreamed of."

We set up a connection call for the next week. I hired her on the spot.

THE LAND OF PLENTY

Money Breakthrough Questions

Who are the most influential and unforgettable people in your life and what lessons around money did you learn from each of them?

Do you feel like you are open to recognizing the need for change? Why or why not?

Have you ever had an awakening? If so, what were the circumstances and what did it take for you to recognize it as such?

Where in your life have you trusted your intuition? What were the results? Are there times you have not trusted your intuition? What was the result?

Part Three

Transforming Your Relationship with Money

Chapter Seven

Leaving the Land of Scarcity

Investments in Unlearning

Over the next six months I worked with Priscilla to create All the Details 2.0. The plan was to hire a team that was energetically aligned so I could free up some time and space and give myself some breathing room. I was excited to create the next version of my business, but apprehensive that I would find the right person I so desperately needed.

I was fascinated to learn that Priscilla works in the Akashic Records, which are like a library that contains every book of who your soul has been and will be through every lifetime. The Records are an extremely powerful tool to help you find your life purpose and discover your next steps with ease. She's a super-savvy business coach, and when she combines her practical business coaching with soul-driven guidance she receives from the Akashic Records, the results are phenomenal.

My first homework was to come up with my mission, vision and values. In order to attract the right person to hire, I had to define what my company was all about. As I started to dig deep for what I wanted for my business and how I wanted to change the world, it soon became obvious that All the Details had a sister company who wanted to come into the world. And so, **The Money Empowerment Project®** was born. I had no idea what it would look like, or what I would do with it, but I knew it was a *hellavalot* more than just book-keeping. I bought the URL and started sketching out a web-site.

After a couple of months, I was ready to hire and determined to do it differently than the last time. I created a job des-cription that included everything I dreamed of having.

> *While number crunching is the medium, we support entrepreneurs in growth and empowerment to help them experience the freedom that comes with understanding and making money.*
>
> *We're looking for an individual who is:*
> - *Able to trust your intuition and read beyond the numbers*
> - *Not afraid to talk about money in a down-to-earth way*
> - *An analytical thinker with an out-of-the-box approach*

"You are going to ask for an intuitive bookkeeper?" a friend in the financial world exclaimed when she read the posting. "That's brave!"

But if I had learned anything, it was that you had to ask the Universe for what you want *and be specific.*

I had a lead on someone who was related to my family, but I didn't know very well. She had a degree in accounting, and I heard she might be interested in doing some part-time bookkeeping work. The day I was going to post the job des-cription, I was waiting for an appointment and had a couple of minutes to kill. I randomly went on Facebook and the very first thing I saw was a post from her. *Any ideas of how I can make some extra money and ideally work from home?*

I interviewed Lynsey the next week and hired her imme-diately.

Working with Priscilla brought me much more than just a

new employee. I created All the Details 2.0—an entirely new business and an entirely new way of life. To do so, I had to listen to my own intuition and trust the process. I had to invest in myself. I had to unlearn my beliefs about how I should run my business, make money, and evaluate what was important.

I said yes to a lot of things that year. I signed up for Money Bootcamp by Denise Duffield-Thomas (aka Lucky Bitch). She is one of my all-time favorites when it comes to money mindset work. I went to New Jersey for a retreat about creating time and freedom in my business and signed up for another retreat in Costa Rica about global presence and visibility. I also worked one-on-one with Angella, the host of Ignite, on creating transformational events and designing both of my websites.

I spent a lot of money, and I am so glad I did. While I may have been able to do some of this on my own, I certainly would not have gotten to where I wanted to be as fast or as accurately without these investments. Investing in myself has paid off several times over in both money and time. I deliberately chose to invest and make a change.

I also invested in things that would save me time in my personal life. I already had a housekeeper every other week, but I hired a landscaper, and a personal trainer who also prepared some of our weekly meals. Freeing up personal time was critical in creating more space for me in my business. It also gave me the opportunity to have true down time when I wasn't working.

Side note: If you earn more than $20 an hour, there is no reason for you to be doing things you can hire out for that rate (like clean your own house or yard work), unless it is something you truly enjoy. Why spend five or six hours cleaning your house and pulling weeds when you could be making money during that time? This is true for household tasks *and* smaller tasks within your business. Investing in things that save you time is worth every penny.

What really shifted for me in this time of expansion and growth was that I opened up to new points of view. When I look back and connect the dots Steve Jobs-style, I see leaving the Land of Scarcity meant focusing on myself rather than focusing on my clients. For years, I believed that focusing on what my client—or my boss—had hired me to do was the only way for me to succeed. In order to unlearn these stories and patterns, I had to invest in myself in ways I never considered before: hiring a coach, going on retreats, hiring out household tasks. To unlearn working REALLY HARD also meant learning how to receive. I had to do my work and my life in a completely new way.

> *"When I let go of what I am,*
> *I become what I might be."*
> *– John Heider*

Get Out of Your Own Way and Start Receiving

Sometimes we have to get out of our head and out of our own way to receive. Receiving takes a mindset shift as much as it does deliberate choice.

As women, we are taught to not ask for things we want and to be grateful for what we have (which implies we shouldn't want for more). We often give way more than we receive and most of us have not learned the art of receiving with ease.

Receiving is a form of opening yourself up to new possibilities. It's not always easy, but the Land of Plenty is all about new possibilities.

Let me explain what I mean. When I finally hired Lynsey to help ease my workload, I was terrified to tell my clients. I was worried they would think I was abandoning them. Deep down, I was still worried that everything I had worked hard to build would fall apart.

The story I told myself could not have been further from the truth. By hiring her, I have more impact in the world and help more people. And because her skills are different than mine and complement what I provide, I am actually giving my clients more value.

It took a few months not only to get her up to speed, but also to learn how to receive help from her. Even though I trusted her entirely, I could feel myself not wanting to give up control. This is probably the biggest self-sabotaging pattern that comes up for me. When I get a new client it often takes me a month or two, or more, to pass them off to my staff. I admit I'm still working on my *I have to work HARD to earn money* story. Yes, it gets easier with time, but I am here to tell you, these money stories are deeply ingrained in us. What makes it easier is knowing the story to look for and recognizing the patterns when they come up. I can spot my story in about five seconds, and the more I see it and recognize it, the faster I am able to move through it and receive.

I have seen it so many times in my own life and in my clients' lives. We block ourselves from receiving that very thing we want. It might be out of fear of failure or even fear of success, or it might be because we are sabotaging the outcome because we don't believe in the possibility.

I had wanted to break through the six-figure ceiling since year two of being in business. I kept working SO HARD to make it happen and it just felt like I was digging myself deeper and deeper into a hole and recreating the Matrix I had left behind when I entered the entrepreneurial world. My income would creep up each month, but so would the number of hours I was working.

Then came my amazing year of coaching and expansion. And

it happened. What's so crazy was that the more I stopped working hard, the easier it became to make money. When I hit my six-figure goal, to my surprise and delight, it didn't happen by working hard. It happened by letting go, getting out of my own way, and allowing myself to receive help. Breaking through the six-figure ceiling was a direct result of investing in myself, unlearning the stories that no longer served me, and being open to change. Not only do I now make more money, but I work less *and* help more people.

Remember, this is not just about receiving money, but also receiving time and help. In the Land of Plenty, sometimes what you are asking for shows up in unexpected ways, so stay open and aware.

Finding Your WHY

One of the keys to finding abundance is defining what you want and claiming it. You have to believe it is possible *and* make a deliberate choice to step into the possibility. To do so, it really helps to know your WHY.

If your goal is to make a $250,000 per year, ask yourself WHY? What is your ultimate goal? What is that money going to provide for you? Here are some examples of powerful WHYs:
- To be debt-free
- Own your own home
- Put your kids through college
- Travel to bucket list destinations
- Quit your job and work on your business full-time
- Feel secure
- Retire by the age of 50

Your WHY is whatever really lights you up.

In order to feel abundant, you first have to **define what abundance looks like to you**. It is different for everyone. It might be a certain amount in your bank account, or a certain amount you earn each year. It might not be monetary. It might be having the time and freedom to travel, or spending time with family.

Give yourself permission to dream. I like to think of this like Desire Mapping for money. If you are unfamiliar with this concept, Danielle LaPorte created *The Desire Map*, and the idea is that rather than setting goals based on an arbitrary marker of success, you define your goals based on how you want to *feel*.

So many people think that money is going to solve all their problems, but they don't take the time to really think about how they want to *feel* once they have money. Money for money's sake often leaves people feeling empty and un-fulfilled. Most people aren't actually chasing money, they are chasing a feeling like security or freedom. For me, the feelings that resonate most are spaciousness and expansiveness.

Reconnecting with My WHY

My Aunt Ginger is an amazing healer. Since I was a little girl, I have loved being around her and her energy. We have always lived in different cities, so I was not particularly close with her, but the connection between us is undeniable.

Her main healing modality is Reconnective Healing, a form of energy work. I had been intrigued about doing a Personal Reconnection, which is a two-day process that accelerates your soul's evolution by reconnecting you to the Universe and who you are through all of your lifetimes. Yes, it is totally *"woo,"* but the process spoke to me.

I finally did a Reconnection the week before the Ignite event, and when we finished the process, she joked, "Remember today's date—4/20. That should be easy to remember because it is 'pot day.' A year from now I want you to ask people how you have changed."

I started seeing the number 420 everywhere—from numbers on bank statements, to the time on the clock, to license plates in front of me. The numbers seemed to appear every time I turned around. It was like the angels were talking to me, telling me I was on the right path.

Within the next weeks and months, so much in my life started to shift. I felt like I had activated *magic* in my life. People I needed to meet started showing up. I was part of conversations I needed to hear. Emails would appear in my inbox with opportunities I had never considered before. The shift was a direct result of asking questions and being open to possibility. **Questioning everything from this place of possibility allowed me to reconnect with my WHY.**

As my business started to transform from asking questions and seeking out what was possible, I began to apply the same technique to my life.

What do I really want my life to look like?
Is my hard work getting me closer to my dream life?
Why do I feel like I have to work so hard?
What is my WHY in my personal life?

Once the answers were clear, the changes I had been asking for started to show up. But not necessarily in a straight line.

My husband worked with my stepdad in his electrical contracting business. Yes, the same one my stepdad ran out of our basement while I was growing up. Not much had changed in 40 years. The business was still in the basement. The initial plan was for Brian to take over the business so my stepdad could retire. After several years without any discussion of how the transition would happen, my husband was miserable in the daily grind.

We were both working SO HARD and while we were "successful," neither one of us was finding much joy. One day, we were talking about our work/life balance, and we took a step back and asked ourselves, WHY are we working so hard? What is the end goal?

We knew we didn't want to retire in Utah. Neither of us loved the winters or the snow. We had dreamed about moving to San Diego for over a decade to enjoy the sun and live close to a few of our family members that lived there. After much discussion and asking lots of questions about what we wanted our future to look like, we decided to approach my stepdad about selling the business and take a *huge* leap. We were ready to move.

Letting Things Fall Apart

As scary as it can be, letting go of things that no longer serve you is necessary if you want things to change. Even if that means letting go of everything that is comfortable and familiar. Letting things fall apart gives you the space you need to reach what is possible and experience the Land of Plenty.

We decided to list our house in December. Although December is traditionally a horrible time to list a house, it was great for us because we weren't 100 percent sure we were ready to make the move, and it would be a good time to test the market. We listed it high, knowing that we weren't in any rush to sell. When the timing was right, it would happen.

We hired a good friend as our agent and put up the for-sale sign on December 8. Typically, he'll have an open house the first weekend he lists a house, but that weekend was his wife's birthday and their anniversary, so he asked to move it to the following week, *December 16*. Immediately, I knew we would sell the house that day—it was the one-year anniversary of my grandfather passing away. I knew Bill was busy wielding his angelic superpowers to make it all come together.

The morning of December 16, I booked myself a massage to

get out of the way of the open house and pamper myself on what was going to be an emotional day of anniversaries and change. As my intuition predicted, we received an offer: Cash. Nearly full price. A buyer willing to rent back to us until we found something new.

The plan was to close right away. Shortly after signing the initial papers, however, our agent called. "Are you willing to wait until after the first of the year to close? The buyer would like to wait to move some money around."

"Of course – no problem."

Immediately I knew we would close on my grandma's birthday, January 9. I knew my grandparents were both re-arranging the stars to make everything fall into place.

We were scheduled to close on Monday, January 8, one day before her birthday. On that Sunday afternoon, our beloved 19-year-old cat Kosmo had a stroke. We rushed him to the emergency vet and the prognosis wasn't good. We had to make the heart-wrenching decision to let him go. Instead of closing on Monday, we spent the day at the vet saying good-bye.

There were lots of tears in our house that week. Not just for the loss of our dear cat, but from the sheer uncertainty. *What were we doing?* We even questioned whether or not we should close on the house.

The house felt so empty without Kosmo and my grandfather. Although it felt as if our life was in a tailspin of grief and everything was falling apart at the seams, this space of unknowing allowed for what came next.

We closed on the house the following day, on my grandma's birthday.

Two days later, a house that seemed to be a perfect fit came up on the market in San Diego and we decided to make an offer. The funds from the sale of our house had just been transferred into the bank and we were able to verify the cash we needed to qualify for the loan.

There were multiple offers on the property, as is usually the case in Southern California, and we didn't get the house. Someone else had offered more and was willing to purchase the house without an inspection. We decided to bow out, but the process brought us one step closer.

A week later, another house came up on the market. The house had lots of potential, but I wasn't sure if it was *the one*.

My husband's aunt and cousin live in San Diego and they went to the open house for us and we Facetimed as they walked through the house. We loved the layout and the way the house was positioned on the lot with a fantastic pool and an unobstructed view.

We made an offer without stepping foot into the space.

Ours wasn't the highest offer, but since we already had all of our cash verified and a pre-approved mortgage, we could close the fastest. They accepted our offer. We were scheduled to go to San Diego that Thursday to look for houses anyway, so we scheduled the inspection for Friday.

The house needed some updating including a new kitchen and lots of paint. Thinking that we didn't have the time or the money to remodel the kitchen, we hesitated.

"I know a great company that does kitchen remodels in a couple of weeks for a reasonable price," our agent said.

So we kept moving forward. **During the process, every time I saw something that looked like a roadblock, a solution immediately appeared.** Over the weekend we found all of the contractors we needed for the kitchen and the painting—with a timeline to complete all the work in three weeks. If you've ever worked with contractors, you know this kind of speed is far from the norm.

For me, one big goal of the move was to find a space where my business could really grow and become all that it wanted to be. Priscilla suggested walking into the space that would be my office and asking the room if it would create more. When I walked into one of the bedrooms that faced the pool, the answer was a resounding *YES.*

We closed 10 days later.

The people who sold us the house rented back from us for the next four weeks to give them time to move out. On February 28, we received the keys and moved three weeks later—into a freshly painted home with a brand-new kitchen. And we'd coordinated it all from nearly 1,000 miles away, not to mention I went to Costa Rica for a business retreat in these three weeks as well!

The experience of selling and finding our new house was surreal. Everything fell into place so perfectly, but we had to let it all fall apart and trust in the process in order to allow it to unfold. There were so many times I could have told myself why it couldn't or shouldn't happen. I very easily could have stopped it from happening out of fear of the unknown.

You are crazy to move to California. It's so expensive there.

You won't qualify for a mortgage because you are self-employed.

The "smart thing" to do is stay in Utah where it is cheaper and you have friends.

All of the worries I kept hearing in my head (and from others) could have stopped me in my tracks. But they didn't. I believed in what was possible and I believed in my dream.

Transformation happens when we allow it to happen. It takes saying yes to things that scare the shit out of us. It also takes saying no when *that* scares the shit out of us.

We sold our house not knowing what would come next. We let everything we knew fall apart, trusting it would work out. Looking back, it's amazing to see how the dots connect and I'm sometimes shocked we got to San Diego. I can't believe we had the guts to do it.

The Space Between

The summer before we moved to San Diego, my husband and I took an end of season trip down to Lake Powell with some friends. It was right as my business and life were really starting to transform, and while I could see where I wanted to go, there was a lot of stress around the unknown and how it would all work out.

We slept out under the stars on our boat each night. I am an early-to-bed kind of girl, so in typical fashion I headed off to bed way before the campfire died down. As I was drifting off to sleep, I looked up at the expansive stars you can really only see when you are out in the middle of nowhere. The moon was bright, and thousands of stars danced and spark-led above me. It was pretty spectacular.

About 3:00 am I woke up and what was before me was jaw-dropping. It was full-on Milky Way. The thousands of stars had turned into millions and I felt like I was in the middle of them all. Having grown up in Utah, I've always been surrounded by amazing natural beauty. And while I've seen lots of stars in my life, nothing can come close to what I saw that pre-dawn morning. I lay there, floating in a gorgeous sea of magic, gently rocking with the lapping water below, and a thick blanket of stars above me.

The moon had set and the sun was yet to rise—we were literally in the space between. In my dreamy state, I started to analyze what was before me. It struck me how incredibly awesome it is that such a beautiful, dramatic thing like the Milky Way is always right in front of us. It is just over-shadowed (or should I say over-lit) by the sun or the moon and the hustle of everyday life. Maybe my beautiful life is right there, and I just have to relax and wait for it to be made visible.

If you allow yourself to relax, sometimes that space between can provide the most spectacular and profound moments. You have to allow yourself to be ok with not knowing what comes next and not worry about the moon or the sun.

The Land of Plenty is often discovered in this space between. You give up control and let things fall apart so you can open space for what is new and build the 2.0 version. It can be incredibly uncomfortable, but if you allow yourself to sit in this space, you can see the beauty and possibility around you.

In my office, I have a saying hanging on my wall with a sketch of a sailboat in the background.

Sometimes in the winds of change we find our new direction.

I bought this right after I was fired and was starting up my business. It has served as a guiding principle for just about every stage of my business and my life since.

Living the Dream

The weekend after we moved, my husband and I went to the beach for dinner. As we came over the hill and I saw the Pacific for the first time as an official "California Girl," I nearly wept, my heart was so filled with gratitude. I had wanted to live by the ocean my entire life, and here I was, finally living my dream.

I was so proud that I had followed my heart, despite all the very good excuses I could have used to "play it safe" and stay where it was familiar. I was so grateful I had built a company that allowed me to work from anywhere, and so grateful I had finally understood that life is so much more than working REALLY HARD. **And incredibly grateful that I had restructured my business in a way that allowed me to receive more and live my dream.**

It took unlearning, letting go, and stepping into possibility to live my dream. Was it scary? Hell yes. Was it worth it? Absolutely.

There Are No Accidents

About a week after moving in, I was taking some empty boxes out to the garage when I looked up and noticed a large "420" spray-painted in white on the garage wall.

"Brian, come look at this!" I yelled. "Why is there a 420 is on the wall?"

He walked into the garage and replied, "Honey, it doesn't say 420. It says *H-2-O*. It's just showing where the water shutoff is located."

"Maybe. Maybe not," I said. I stayed in the garage and kept looking at it. And since that day, every time I walk into the garage, I am reminded of the magic that brought me to San Diego. One of the lines on the H is missing and it looks just like a 4. Coincidence? Highly unlikely. After all, there are no accidents.

Money Breakthrough Questions

Do you feel you are investing in yourself enough? If yes, what have been the best investments you have made? Where do you think you need to invest more?

How hard do you feel you work? How much do you work on yourself? Do you feel this is in balance? Why or why not? Anything that needs to shift?

Where do you need to get out of your own way to allow something to fall into place? What is holding you back? What needs to shift?

Where do you feel you are blocking receiving? Why do you think you are blocking what you want?

What is your WHY? If money were no object, how would your life be different? What would you do every day? Where would you live? What do you want your life to look like?

Do you feel what you are doing on a daily basis is getting you closer to your WHY? If not, what needs to shift?

What are the words that describe how you want to feel every day?

What needs to fall apart in your life to make space for something new? Are you willing to let this happen and take deliberate action? Why or why not?

Chapter Eight

Living In the Land of Plenty

What would be possible if you believed there was plenty and never feared there wasn't enough? Think about this for a moment. How much time do you spend in scarcity thinking?

I truly believe that the Land of Plenty exists—and it's right in front of our eyes, just like the Milky Way. It just takes a shift in our perception to see it, create it, and live it.

To live in the Land of Plenty, there are certain beliefs we embody and embrace.
- We believe that money is infinite.
- We stop chasing money because it only makes it run.
- We know that money multiplies; it doesn't disappear.
- We believe it all counts!
- We're clear on our perception of plenty.
- We're grateful for what we have.
- We recognize our money journey.
- We trust ourselves.
- We celebrate.
- We learn how to truly receive.
- We know what plenty is, and we aren't afraid to uplevel our dreams.

We Believe That Money Is Infinite

Money is infinite. Do you believe this? The first time I heard this phrase, it blew my mind. I was having a conversation with my sister-in-law when she said, *"There's plenty of money out there—you just have to go out and make it."*

What do you mean there is plenty of money? How can money be infinite when I just make this small paycheck twice a month? My money felt so predetermined and limited.

Being plugged into the Matrix, I believed there was a designated amount of money I could make, and I was stuck in that tiny little box. How much I made was determined by my boss, and if it wasn't my boss, it was my boss's boss, and if it wasn't my boss's boss, it was predetermined by the choices I had made when I decided what college I would go to, what degree I would earn, and what jobs I applied for. It was predetermined before I was born. Sure, there were others in this world with great wealth, but that was for others. Not for me.

Infinite money felt like a legend. Something you hear about and dream about but never really believe exists. Before she said those words, I had never thought about *really* being in control over how much money I could make. Not once.

But the exciting news for all of us is *it's absolutely true*. Money *is* infinite. There is plenty of money out there. There are plenty of ways to make money. Money multiplies and regenerates (I will talk more about this in a bit). But first, you need to figure out what is standing in your way of *believing* money is infinite. Talk about eye-opening!

We Stop Chasing Money Because It Only Makes It Run

Have you ever tried so hard (again and again) to make a sale or get a raise, and nothing ever changes? When other people seem to have things come to them so easily, do you wonder *why can't that be me*?

If you really dissect what is going on behind the scenes in both these scenarios, without a shadow of a doubt, I can tell you the law of attraction is at play.

The law of attraction is the concept that like energies are attracted to one another. You think a negative thought, and something negative is going to happen. You think a positive thought, and something positive will happen. While the results don't happen overnight, the law of attraction is just like gravity, pulling what you put out there towards you. The more you focus on the positive energy around money, the more money will appear.

Your thoughts, feelings and beliefs create your reality. If you are constantly saying "I can't afford that," guess what? You probably won't be able to afford it.

In order for the law of attraction to work its magic, you have to really believe it. And I mean down to your core and in your soul. For instance, you can't say in one breath *"I am an abundant being,"* and then constantly complain about how your clients never pay you on time.

Believing and embodying this concept takes time and practice and mindfulness.

If you are chasing after money and feeling like it is out of reach, stop chasing it because it only makes it run.

I realize this is much easier said than done. Remember, we are programmed to believe we need to hustle to achieve. But hustling and chasing are based in fear. Fear there is not enough. Fear that money will never come to you unless you work really hard. Fear that if you don't do it all perfectly, you'll lose everything. And you know what? Fear is a negative emotion that negatively affects your money.

Now, I'm not saying sit back and do nothing and the money will magically appear. It does take some deliberate action. But the difference is in the energy and approach behind the action. The biggest shift in my business, my money, and my ability to afford my dreams came when I really started to grasp this concept. When I stopped worrying that my pricing was too high, or I had to be a certain way, or have a certain balance in my bank account, or provide a certain thing in order to attract clients, everything changed.

Most of all, I stopped being afraid.

I started focusing on everything that was positive in my life and my business. I acknowledged the abundance that was right in front of me. I showed gratitude for every single client, and every single dollar that came into my bank account. I recognized my skills and superpowers as wonderful tools instead of judging myself and thinking I should have or be more.

Acknowledging where money is showing up—even the smallest amounts—and being grateful for what you have is the first step in making the law of attraction work for you.

Once you stop chasing money, you open yourself up to being in the flow to receive money.

We Know that Money Multiplies; It Doesn't Disappear

Try this: Think of money as something bigger than yourself and what is in your bank account. Now consider that as money moves, it doesn't disappear; instead, it multiplies and flows.

Say I have $100 and I give it to my friend Stephanie for cutting my hair. In the Land of Scarcity, I would feel like I just gave away my $100 and it was gone. But in the Land of Plenty, I recognize the $100 still exists. It is in Stephanie's bank account. And she is going to spend that $100 on a couple of concert tickets. The concert venue then spends the $100 on advertising with a local magazine, the same local magazine that happens to be my client. I do some book-keeping for the magazine, and the $100 comes back to me. That same $100 has now become income four times over for four different people. This is what I mean when I say money multiplies each time it changes hands.

If you trust in the flow and realize how much money is out there, it is simply a matter of time and making some deli-berate choices before that money you "spent" comes back to you.

My favorite emoji on my phone is the money with angel wings 💸. I love to imagine money coming in and going out like a feather happily dancing in the wind.

While it might feel like money is scarce at times, I want to assure you there is plenty of money out there. Are you open to receiving it? Keep in mind it might be right in front of you and coming to you in unexpected ways.

We Believe It All Counts!

One of my clients is a coach who teaches about what is "crazy possible." She likens the Universe to Amazon. You tell the Universe you want something; it takes your order and it delivers. If you aren't specific, you might not like what shows up. If you really wanted a medium red t-shirt, but just told Amazon you wanted a red shirt, you would receive a red shirt, but it might be a golf shirt. And it might be an XL.

The Universe is no different. You have to be specific with what you want. If you say "Universe, I want more money," chances are you *are* getting more money, it just might be those pennies you find on the ground, or the refund check from your utility company for $3.67.

Be bold in what you ask the Universe to deliver. Be specific.

There is plenty of money out there, and trust me, the Universe wants to give it to you. You have to ask and be willing to receive.

You might be generating abundance in ways you have not yet acknowledged.
- The generous parents or a favorite aunt who gives you gifts each year.
- Credit card points you can redeem for free flights.
- The friend who always buys you lunch.
- That lease you negotiated so you have discounted rent month after month.

In the Land of Plenty these all count. Money and abundance are everywhere. If you start looking around, you might be surprised. Keep in mind, it's not just cash and nothing is too small or too big.

The first time I started looking for and tracking *everything* I received I was shocked. Here I was, asking the Universe for six-figures and it was already there and then some! It was just showing up in lots of different ways other than cash. Within one month, I received almost $5,000 in free or discounted items—everything from marketing money to grow my business from a vendor, redeeming credit card points for cash, discounts on products I use every month, friends treating me to dinner, and redeeming gift cards I had forgotten about. All of these things have *value*. I just wasn't counting them.

No wonder I wasn't seeing an increase in my business income—I already had what I was asking for, I just had not acknowledged it. I realized I needed to ask for more and be specific!

You might discover that you are compartmentalizing money by thinking only your paycheck or income from your business counts. Sometimes money presents itself as opportunity, sometimes as discarded or ignored resources, and other times it is literally cash in the pocket of an old jacket you haven't worn in years.

Most of us have money sitting right in front of us and don't even realize it is there. Don't believe me? Let's go find it! One of my favorite exercises that Denise Duffield-Thomas uses is called Treasure Hunting and it is a game-changer. Take 15 minutes and look around your house for things like loose change and bills, gift cards you haven't used, items that need to be returned for a refund, and checks you forgot to cash. It can be ANYTHING that has value. Total it all up.

After you search for what is already right in front of you, the next step is to look at what could be created with just a little effort. Some ideas to get you going….

- Client leads—is there someone you need to call or email?
- Do you have new programs, products or offerings that are done or mostly done or just need to be advertised or put on your website?
- Is it time to raise your rates or ask your boss for a raise?
- What skills do you have to create money right now?
- Is there a way to make some passive income?
  - Do you have something you can rent?
  - Do you have some extra money you could invest somewhere?
- Look at your expertise—what can you make into a leveraged or evergreen product without a lot of time or effort?
- Is there a new offering that wants to be created?
- Where is money already in your life?

THEY ALL COUNT! Each and every time I do this exercise, I am amazed at what I uncover.

Did you do it? Are you starting to feel like you live in the Land of Plenty? I hope so, because we are just getting started!

We're Clear on Our Perception of Plenty

So, I have a feeling you are closer than you think to living an abundant life. As I've said, it takes a shift in perspective to redefine our reality. This shift happens when you have the **perception of plenty**.

I touched on perception in an earlier chapter and want to expand on it here. Remember, abundance is a feeling—not a destination. Anyone, regardless of how much money they have or don't have, can feel scarcity or abundance.

So much of your relationship with money is about your mindset and the perception of what you have. If you want to live in the Land of Plenty, you need to put the law of attraction to work and start living abundantly. Stop feeding the fear and scarcity monster.

There are plenty of leads.
There are plenty of clients.
There is plenty of money.
There is plenty of possibility.
There is plenty of everything.

Anything that stands in the way of you believing this comes from a place of lack and fear. Especially in the entrepreneur world, perceptions around plenty can be skewed. You hear lots about how this person was tens of thousands of dollars in debt and climbed her way to a seven-figure business, or how that person made six figures in six months. If we think we should be further ahead or set more aggressive financial goals and we constantly compare ourselves to others, this can skew our perception and feed into the idea that we are lacking.

I used to do triathlons and thought I was a horrible runner. I had a few running friends who consistently would run nine-minute miles. I wanted to be able to run fast with ease—just like they could, but I was pacing around a 10:30 mile. So I started working with a running coach. One of the first things she told me was lots of people would love to have my pace. *Really?* I had been so focused on achieving the illusive 10-minute mile, I never thought about the people who couldn't ever reach an 11-minute mile. The irony is if I went out for a run today, I would be lucky to hit a 12 or 13-minute mile—and it's pretty likely I wouldn't even be able to run a full mile straight without gasping for some serious air.

It is all a matter of perception. How I defined "fast" is similar to how people define "plenty" or "rich." Comparing yourself to others does nothing. There will always be people who are faster than you and there will always be people who are slower. There will always be people who have more and people who have less. The Land of Plenty comes from a personal discovery of what plenty means to you.

We're Grateful for What We Have

Acknowledge everything that comes to you with gratitude. Abundance multiplies with gratitude. This is what I mean when I say abundance is an art. Practice gratitude every day.

All that shame and guilt you have about money—**let it go**. Money won't come to you if you are stressing about it. Fear, avoidance and self-judgment have no place in the Land of Plenty and repel what you seek. Gratitude is incredibly magnetic.

We Recognize Our Money Journey

We are all on a money journey, and this journey is part of our soul work. As we evolve from one money stage to the next, each of these stages provides a soul lesson. To reach the Land of Plenty, we need to acknowledge where we are, and embody and master the concepts that help us grow and evolve.

There are a few stages we all go through to reach the Land of Plenty.

Stage 1 – Fear of scarcity and not enough. You work REALLY HARD, but always seem to fall short. You are held back by over-analyzing, rehashing the past, beating yourself up for past mistakes or not being enough. You feel intense guilt and shame. The soul lesson in this stage is to understand what abundance means for you.

Stage 2 – Fear of unsustainability. You earn more than enough but worry that you can't sustain it. You are held back by feeling like you have to do everything yourself and you are overwhelmed with exhaustion. You need to be in control because you fear everything will fall apart. The soul lesson in this stage is to find wholeness.

Stage 3 – Fear of dissatisfaction. You have money, but you don't think it is possible to have money *and* be satisfied at the same time. You are held back by the opinions and projections of others that are ruling your life. You may suffer from imposter syndrome (*Who am I to have money* and *happiness?)* The soul lesson in this stage is to find your worth.

Stage 4 – Fear of being or having too much. You are happy with the money you have but you fear having more. You fear that having more will push you over the edge and you might lose it all. You are held back by thoughts like *"Wanting more would be greedy"* or *"I am fine, no need to rock the boat."* The soul lesson in this stage is to actualize your full potential.

Most people go through these stages in order, but not always. It's ok to be where you are in your journey. We all have different breakthroughs, at different times and for different reasons. Stop judging yourself and comparing yourself to others. Recognize where you are and look for when your money stories and patterns are at play. Take the next step that is right *for you.*

As a bonus, I have created a chart of these stages and tools you can use to conquer these fears.

Money Journey Stages

Stage	Where You Are	What Is Holding You Back	Soul Lesson	Mantra	Embody and Master	Tools
Stage 1 Fear of Scarcity and Not Enough	You work really hard, but you always seem to fall short	Scarcity, over-analyzing, rehashing the past, beating yourself up over past mistakes or not being enough, feelings of guilt and shame	I am enough, I am abundant	I am abundant with money	Abundance	Mindset work, understand your money story
Stage 2 Fear of Unsustainability	You earn more than enough, but you worry you can't sustain it	Thoughts like I have to do everything myself	I am whole and complete	Money supports and energizes me	Wholeness	Asking for help, creating better systems
Stage 3 Fear of Dissatisfaction	You have money, but you don't think you can have money and be satisfied	Letting other's opinions and projections rule your life, Imposter syndrome: who do you think you are to have money and happiness?	I am worthy of designing a life I love	Money is satisfying to me; Money allows me to be all of me and do good in the world	Worth	Mindset work, find your WHY, invest in yourself
Stage 4 Fear of Being or Having Too Much	You have money, but fear having more	Thoughts like "I don't need more, more is greedy. What will people think? I am fine, why rock the boat? The status quo is fine; I've got more than enough."	Permission to actualize full potential	I give myself permission to be wealthy, to have more, and to have plenty	Full Potential	Learn to receive, up level your dreams, invest in yourself

We Trust Ourselves

One day, back in my early 20s, I was stressed about paying some bills.

As I was telling my dad about my anxiety, he asked, "Have you ever been in a position where you could not pay the bills?" I paused for a second and responded, "No."

"Then give yourself the gift to stop stressing about it and trust you will figure it out."

It stopped me in my tracks. Deep down, I knew this was true. I had been making money since my early teens and I'd never gone without. I knew I had the tenacity to make things happen. Even if it meant I had to work three jobs (which, luckily, I never had to do), I would figure out a way to make the money I needed. It was the first time I acknowledged that I could make money appear when I need it.

A huge stress lifted. And guess what? When you lighten your stress around money, things get a bit easier.

Sometimes it just takes a little trust in yourself to make a shift.

We Celebrate

Celebration is a very powerful tool when it comes to finding the Land of Plenty.

Celebrating your money successes is the ultimate law of attraction at work. Because it turns something that is often negative and fear-based into something that is joyful, it helps transform your relationship with money.

Each time you celebrate a money success—no matter how big or small—you take a baby step towards your dream.

We live in a fast-paced world and so many of us (myself included) move on to the next task before really acknowledging the success and transformation that is happening in our lives every day. To live in the Land of Plenty, stop and celebrate.

Celebrate every time you hit a milestone.
Celebrate every time you launch a new product even though you were afraid.
Celebrate every time you recognize a pattern that is holding you back.
Celebrate when you add someone on your team who supports you.
Celebrate every time you get a new client.
Celebrate every time you reach a goal.

How you celebrate is up to you. I love to splurge on a day at the spa or a night out eating delicious food. It doesn't really matter how you celebrate, as long as you are acknowledging the success, because doing this encourages more of the same to show up.

We Learn How to Truly Receive

Earlier, I told you why it was important to get out of your own way in order to receive. Now I want to go a little deeper into the topic of receiving. After all, how many times have you asked the Universe to send you something and not recognized it when it showed up?

It's like the old joke:

There is a big storm and a preacher is on his knees praying for God to save him. As the waters fill the street, one of his neighbors comes by in a canoe. "Jump in, the waters are rising."

The preacher replies "No, I am sure God will save me."

The waters continue to rise and the first story of his

house is under water. He goes to the second story and looks out the window. A rescue boat comes by. "Jump in, I can take you to safety."

"No," the preacher replies "God will save me."

The waters get higher so he climbs to his roof. A helicopter shows up and throws him a ladder. "Climb in!" the pilot yells.

"No—God will save me."

Inevitably he drowns and when he goes to heaven, he asks God why he didn't save him from the flood.

God replies, "I sent you two boats and a helicopter— what more did you want?"

Do you block what is coming to you because it doesn't look or feel like what you expected? Are you blocking what the Universe wants to send you because you aren't open to receiving?

I know it sounds ridiculous on the surface that you would block *good* things from coming your way, but many times our unconscious mind tells us stories about how we don't deserve it, or it can't be that easy, or such good things only happen to other people.

This is where our money stories and perceptions really rise to the surface and why it is so critical to understand them for what they are—*just stories*.

We may feel unworthy on some level; for me it usually shows up when I have easy money coming my way and I don't feel I have worked hard enough to earn it.

Sometimes you might feel like you don't have the time or energy to receive. It could be that you need to spend a little bit of time restructuring some of your business systems so you can expand and take on more clients, but instead of spending the time to implement these changes, you keep spinning your wheels in the daily grind.

My advice? Get out of your own way!

In the first few months of moving to San Diego I was feeling incredibly uninspired. All of a sudden, I *had* everything I had worked so hard for. All my dreams had come true. I almost felt like I was out of dreams, and I wasn't sure if I could or wanted to dream any bigger. #firstworldproblems.

I had leveled up big time and I was left with this over-whelming feeling of *Now What?* Not that I wasn't grateful for what I had accomplished, because I certainly was. It was more like I had checked off everything on my bucket list and I was left without any goals to achieve.

It was uncomfortable.

It took me several months before I settled into my new normal. Bottom line: it was about my feeling of worth. I had to get out of my own way and accept that I was worthy to receive it all and integrate everything that comes with receiving.

Sometimes it takes courage to take the next step, to uplevel and dream bigger, because it might mean you need to change. You might think you want the dream, but in order to receive it, you may need to change your systems; de-clutter some old beliefs or habits; or even let go of unhealthy clients, patterns, or relationships.

Learning to truly receive is not for the faint of heart. It takes some pretty deep soul work coupled with strategies, which I'll talk about in the bonus chapter. But on the other side is the Land of Plenty and it is beautiful and abundant and so worth the effort.

We Know What Plenty Is, and We Aren't Afraid to Uplevel Our Dreams

I was recently at the grocery store with a friend buying some items for a BBQ.

"I just wish I could buy strawberries and not think about the price," she said as she picked up and examined a box of plump, glistening berries. To be perfectly honest, I have never paid attention to the price of strawberries, or the price of gas for that matter. If I need it, I buy it. But she reminded me that lots of people don't live that way.

To know if you have made it to the Land of Plenty, you first have to define what *plenty* looks like for you. "Plenty" might be something as small as not paying attention to the cost of groceries. It might be moving into a new house in a better neighborhood, being able to send your kid to private school, or buying a yacht and sailing around the world for a year.

The Land of Plenty is made up of anything you are willing to dream about. Just keep in mind that no matter how big or small your dreams may be, the way to stay in the Land of Plenty is to live in a state of constant gratitude.

When you achieve your dream and level up, your new reality becomes the norm. Gratitude is the only way to create more of the same.

A few of my friends were recently in town and we were hanging out by my pool on a Tuesday morning. One had a conference call she had to be on, but she was determined to get in some pool time as well. So, she put on her swimsuit, put in her ear buds and sat waist deep in the water while she was on her call. No one on the call had any idea she was lounging in a pool. And that is totally ok.

At one point while she was on mute she looked at me and said, "Damn, I need to up my dreams." I just had to smile. Everything is possible in the Land of Plenty. How big you can dream?

Money Breakthrough Questions

Do you believe money is infinite? Why or why not? What is or has been standing in your way of believing money is infinite?

Are you chasing money? What can you do to stop making it run?

Where have you been discounting money or value? Do you need to change what you are asking the Universe to deliver?

What did you learn from searching for things of value? What did you find? Did it change the way you view the amount of abundance in your life?

What does your Land of Plenty look like? How would you define *enough*?

What stage of the money journey do you think you are in? What is your soul lesson?

What would be possible if you truly trusted yourself with money?

How are you going to celebrate your money successes?

Do you feel like you have an issue receiving? How does this show up?

Where do you need to uplevel your dreams?

Chapter Nine

Why Your Money Empowerment Matters

I have a dream that everyone can find joy, possibility and abundance through money empowerment. This isn't just my personal goal, but a dream for a world where *everyone* lives in the Land of Plenty.

> *My vision is for a world where women entrepreneurs are inspired to rise up and embrace their money power. Women who understand their relationship with money change the world.*

Our world, now more than ever, needs conscious people who care. We need these conscious, caring people to make a difference through their interactions with money. Imagine if all of the good, caring, conscious people of the world had money and spent it on things they cared about, supporting their own micro-communities and donating to their favorite causes. What would be different?

Money gives you the ability to make change. **Having money puts you in a place of power to make the world a better place.** When you embrace your money power and make a conscious effort to have a better relationship with money, you are taking the first step. Deep down to my core, the WHY around the Money Empowerment Project® is to create worldwide sisterhoods where we support each other. Powerful women, consciously and joyfully, spending and receiving from one another in micro-communities, knowing there is Plenty.

At Ignite, the event where I had my awakening, there were only two men in the room. On the last morning, one of the men got up and made a very poignant statement. I scribbled it down in my notebook because I didn't want to forget it.

"Men have been in power in this world for a long time, and we have done a pretty crappy job," he said. "It is time for women to take over and run things for a while. It is time for balance."

I believe that the balance of power starts with money empowerment. And it's time for women to do everything it takes to embrace their money power.

If you are a male reading this book, please know I'm not excluding you from this movement. We need you, too. We need your support in bringing equality and balance and harmony to our world. For centuries, women have been not only stuck in the Matrix of the corporate world, but in the Matrix of society, often pigeonholed into roles that pay very little. While secretary, nurse, homemaker and school teacher are all necessary and meaningful roles, the problem is that we as women often don't achieve our full potential because we fear what others will think, we are too busy taking care of others, or we don't have the same opportunities as men do to develop our skills including education and promotions.

It's hard to believe it's almost 2020 and we're still reading stories and statistics like this:

It is quoted in several places that women only apply for a job if they meet 100 percent of the qualifications, while men apply if they meet 60 percent.[3] Women are also traditionally seen as bad negotiators and are called *bossy* or *pushy* when they show their negotiation skills.

According to CNBC, white women make 79 cents to every dollar a man earns,[4] and the stats get worse when you add in women of color.

There are 2,153 billionaires in the world as of March 5, 2019 according to *Forbes.* Of those, only 11 percent or 244 are women.[5]

It is time for women to impact the economy in a conscious way. It is time for women to take ownership, step into leadership, and stop under-charging. It is time women claim our power and know that our value and our worth is infinite.

I hold a big vision for the world, and it starts with women entrepreneurs embracing their money power. Money is and can be expansive. Not just for someone else. For you. For me. For everyone.

How You Spend Your Money Matters

This movement that I am talking about is a complete paradigm shift. It turns the way we look at money and power sideways so we can see it through a different lens.

Remember that money multiplies and regenerates every time it changes hands. When you start to spend your money

---

[3] Harvard Business Review, Web, 30 September, 2019
https://hbr.org/2014/08/why-women-dont-apply-for-jobs-unless-theyre-100-qualified
[4] CNBC, Web, 30 September, 2019
https://www.cnbc.com/2019/04/02/heres-how-much-men-and-women-earn-at-every-age.html
[5] Forbes, Web, 30 September, 2019
https://www.forbes.com/billionaires/#47995725251c

in ways that support and generate money for like-minded business owners, the acreage in the Land of Plenty grows.

If we go back to the example I used, when I spend money on a haircut, my hair stylist in turn spends money at the concert venue, who in turn spends money on advertising with a magazine, who in turn spends money on bookkeeping and so the money multiplies and regenerates back to me.

By doing this, we create micro-communities and micro-economies. The more I spend money supporting my clients' businesses, the more money my clients have to spend with me. Micro-communities can be a source of inspiration and support and these micro-communities can change the world.

The way you spend your money matters. The way you invest your money matters. Your dollars speak volumes. If a business doesn't treat its employees well, stop shopping there. If a company is socially or environmentally irresponsible, stop investing in their stock. This is also money empowerment.

The way you earn your money matters. When we earn money with integrity by providing valuable services and products at a rate that is in alignment with our worth, our customers and clients feel good about spending money and investing in us and our businesses.

Conscious spending, earning, and investing at their core are interactions between people. People with families, and dreams, and hearts. It's not about earning as much as possible at the expense of others. Money is not about fear, greed, or shame. Money is a tool that supports us and our interactions with money can be a win/win for both parties.

When we earn and spend money consciously, we all win because we are investing in each other. We are spending money for things that better ourselves and supporting people who support us.

If we go back to its very origins, money was invented as a tool to help people barter and trade. In today's world it has turned into something that is often objectified and idolized. It defines us. It has been made into something much bigger than it really is. It is time to take money back to its essence. It is time to stop worshiping money for money's sake and use it as the tool it was meant to be.

Big Magic Moments: Co-Creating with the Universe

One of my favorite books is *Big Magic* by Elizabeth Gilbert. She believes creativity taps you on the shoulder with an idea, and if you don't pay attention to it, it will find someone else who will. To illustrate her point, she tells a story about how she was writing a novel with some very specific details. She put it on hold and eventually the novel left her. A few years later she was catching up with a good friend and fellow author who just happened to be writing a novel with the same specific details! They had never discussed the story line. The creative idea left Elizabeth Gilbert since she wasn't nurturing it and moved on to her friend. She ends the story with, "And *that,* my friends, is Big Magic."

Big Magic also happens when ideas start to appear at the same time in many different places. Such collective con-sciousness is the way the Universe works when there is a need for an idea or a movement to come forth into the world. You see this a lot in science: the discovery of oxygen, evolution, calculus, and HIV, the virus that causes AIDS just to name a few.

When you start to see synchronicity happen, pay attention. Don't discount it or think you must be crazy. The Universe is talking to you. The Universe is confirming what you know is true.

I believe right now the Universe is asking for a Big Magic Moment around conscious money and money empowerment. I had one of these moments when I was creating my 21-Day

Money Cleanse. The idea to create a money cleanse came to me in December of 2018. I was just in the beginning stages of writing this book when the idea flew in the window as I was driving down the street. I still can see exactly where I was when the idea came to me—passing Lake Hodges on Del Dios Highway. I knew in that very moment I needed to create a 21-Day Money Cleanse and I needed to get it done in time for the new year and spring cleaning.

The timing was horrible. I had just started writing this book and I had aspirations of getting the book done by spring. Throwing a big project like the money cleanse into the mix was certainly going to derail my timeline. January is also a really busy time for me. I typically have a large event I manage for a long-term client that is in full swing in January, and it is when all of my bookkeeping clients need year-end numbers and tax forms finalized.

But I trusted my intuition, ignored all of the excuses and forged ahead. I also knew that there would be pieces of the cleanse that would feed into this book, and I knew that the book would not feel ignored by me taking this side street.

A few weeks later, I got a text from Priscilla. She was in a bookstore and saw a newly published book called *The 30-Day Money Cleanse* by Ashley Feinstein Gerstley. (Publication date: January 1, 2019.) While I have not read the book, I think it is absolutely fascinating that two people who have never met came up with basically the same idea to be launched into the world around the same time. I am sure she had the idea for this book long before I had my idea for my program since writing a book takes at least a few months if not longer, but the point is, the Universe wanted and needed this information in the world, in a specific way. I was just one of the vehicles to make it happen.

Because I live in the Land of Plenty, I didn't freak out and think I should change the name of my program or scrap the idea all together. I took it as a sign. I launched the 21-Day

Money Cleanse, ran my first successful cleanse, and transformed lives. More than ever, the world needs this information and it needs to come from multiple voices and multiple avenues.

The world is magical if you are open to the signs. Trust the Universe. Ask the Universe for what you want. Follow your intuition. Big Magic is waiting to happen everywhere.

A Place at the Table

As I sit at my pool in San Diego, overlooking my utterly serene view, I am overwhelmed with gratitude. Sometimes I have to stop and ask myself if this is real. What did I do to have my dreams come true?

It's not like this dream life magically appeared. I mean it did, but it didn't. As I said earlier, it took me some time to finally settle in and *receive* all that I had created for myself. I had to figure out how to go from "What now?" to really embodying the idea of "I have arrived." And I am still on this journey.

As I started to write this book, so many times I felt I was "bragging" or suffered from imposter syndrome. *"Who am I to share my story about how to think and feel about money?"* I don't always have all the answers, and I certainly don't have all my shit together every waking moment. There are times I stress about money. There are times when I fall into fear and scarcity. But the more I work on it, the easier it gets to move quickly to the other side.

I just want to be real. The first 18 months in San Diego have had their ups and downs. The sale of my husband's business took longer than we thought, and it took a lot longer than we expected to get into a routine and really get settled in. While we have family here, since we both work at home and don't have kids, our ability to make friends is somewhat limited. (If you live in San Diego and you want some awesome friends with a pool, hit me up!)

The truth is, I don't know it all. I don't know what comes next. I am just listening to the whisperings from the Universe and taking baby steps every day. I am not a money guru, but what I do know is that the more conscious we become about our relationship with money, and how we interact with money, and stay in a place of gratitude, the more it changes the world. And that has been the driving force for me to write this book.

Not too long ago, Denise Duffield-Thomas posted something that really hit home.

> I am a contributor, not a guru. As soon as I gave myself permission to contribute to the conversation of women and money, and not have to be a guru or an expert, then my business became fun. If you really care about a topic, be a contributor. Who cares if you don't know everything? You don't have to be the best to make a difference to someone.

As The Land of Plenty was taking form in my head and tapping me on the shoulder, I kept pushing away the idea, thinking there were other people out there who are already talking about this stuff. I mean how could I ever compare to the Denises, Bari Tesslers, Lynne Twists and the Jen Sinceros of the world?

Why does my voice matter?

And the more I processed this fear, the louder the urge to write this book became.

I keep seeing a vision of a big long table, similar to the table depicted in the Last Supper, but a lot more fun. Around the table are all of the women who talk about money from a place of abundance and plenty. I see Denise, Bari, Lynne, and Jen and many more who have been a contribution to this conversation around women and money. I picture the table shimmering with beautiful dishes and glassware, abundant food, and plenty of wine and chocolate to get us through the evening. I hear laughter and see the candles burning as the inspiring, world-changing conversation carries us through to the wee hours of morning. It's the kind of conversation that feels like catching up with an old girlfriend you haven't seen in years. There is so much excitement and energy in the air. We feed off of the money conversation because it is joyful and fun and full of possibility.

As I finish up this book, I'm taking *my* seat at the table.

And I want you there, too.

The table is big enough for *all* of us who want to be there.

You see, this whole conscious money thing is a *movement*. It's not just a bunch of individual voices and talking heads rambling on about how to make money and get ahead. That's the old way—this is a whole new way of life. The movement is about embracing kindness and showing respect for one another and supporting each other as we grow our businesses. It is about being conscious around our money and not feeding into the fear, money stories and old patterns that keep us from being rich and having wealth. It is about realizing that every time a woman invests in another woman, we create and elevate a micro-community.

Remember how I said in the introduction I felt the Universe was conspiring with me to write this book? Well, I believe that if you have gotten to the end of this book, the Universe is conspiring again—this time to offer you an invitation to take a seat at the table.

So, as you enter the Land of Plenty, leave your scarcity at the door and pull up a chair next to me. We've got a world to change!

Money Breakthrough Questions

Are you ready to rise up and embrace your money power? What does that look like for you?

What is the world you imagine?

Are there any shifts you want to make in how you earn or spend money? What are they and why?

Have you ever been in a micro-community? What was your experience?

Do you see your place at the table? How does it feel? Who is at the table with you? What transformation are you feeling as you sit at the table?

Are you ready to change the world?

CONCLUSION

So, what's next for you and your money? Are you ready to live in the Land of Plenty? I hope by now the answer to that question is a HELL YES!

I have some resources for you. I have included a bonus chapter in which I share my advice from the bookkeeping trenches. These are tried-and-true tips and tricks that help you get your $hit together when it comes to money. It is all the practical advice I share with my bookkeeping clients, day in and day out, including FAQs about hiring a bookkeeper. These tips will help reduce your money stress, which in turn will help you attract more abundance.

After the bonus chapter, you'll find a list of resources—books and courses from people who talk about money the way that I do. Each is a valuable contributor to the money empowerment movement. I recognize that not everyone hears information the same way. While what I have to say might resonate with some of you, for others, a similar message might land better coming from someone else in a slightly different way. In the Land of Plenty this is not a competition. This is about being a voice in the movement where we need as many voices as possible. I am thrilled and honored to make additional suggestions of people who will help you on your money journey.

If what I have to say resonates with you, and you are interested in working with me directly, please visit www.moneyempowermentproject.com for current offerings. I would love to get to know you better and support you on your money empowerment journey. If you are interested in my bookkeeping services, you can visit my website www.all-details.com.

I would also love to hear about any money breakthroughs you've experienced as a result of reading this book. If you want to share your breakthroughs with me, email me at empower@moneyempowermentproject.com or share your breakthrough on the Money Empowerment Project Facebook page.

And let's keep talking. The world needs more conscious money conversations. We need people who share messages of joy, possibility and abundance. We need you. I hope you accept this invitation to rise up and embrace your money power.

Bonus Chapter

Advice from the Bookkeeping Trenches

As a bookkeeper, I have had the honor and privilege of seeing the nitty-gritty details of people and their relationship with money.

By now you know I'm a bit of a Denise Duffield-Thomas junkie. A couple years ago, I took part in a live VIP event in Los Angeles with her. It was fantastic, and an honor to be in the same room with Denise and some of the amazing women who are part of her Lucky Bee community.

As we were discussing the importance of knowing your numbers, the topic of hiring a bookkeeper came up. Another bookkeeper was in the room, and we were discussing the best way to find and work with a bookkeeper. At one point in the discussion, a woman raised her hand and asked, "I know this might sound like a silly question, but what is a bookkeeper?"

Then something jaw-dropping happened. About half the room acknowledged they didn't know what a bookkeeper was, nor why they should hire one. I was dumbfounded. Here I was in a room full of women who were *focused on money* and yet many of them didn't know what a bookkeeper was.

The woman sitting next to me whispered in my ear, "You should write an e-book about this!" And so I began to write this chapter at the airport as I was heading home. I frantically scribbled notes of all the things every entrepreneur needed to know about bookkeepers.

What exactly is a bookkeeper?
A bookkeeper is someone who helps you track all of the transactions that happen in your business. This person may also help you with other things related to finances like payroll, sales tax, invoicing, receiving payments, and paying bills.

Why is bookkeeping important?
Keeping books in your business is important for a few reasons: First, you are required to keep your books so you can file your taxes. Second, by having an accurate set of books, you are privy to some pretty empowering information. For instance, you'll know how much income you brought in, how much you spent, how much profit you're making, and if you're losing money. Many, many business owners don't know these numbers.

What will bookkeeping do for my business?
Trust me, if you have not kept books before now, the simple act of tracking your money will **transform your business**. It is like shining a light into the darkest of caves. All the sudden, the things you never knew were there are staring you in the face. While this can be a scary step for some, I have yet to encounter a single person who has ever regretted the decision. I have seen clients who believed they were a hot mess with money finally let go of their money stress. I have seen clients who were losing money every month and on the verge of throwing in the towel turn everything around and experience their first profitable month.

Bookkeeping allows you to **understand your numbers**—and knowledge is power. Suddenly, you can make decisions about your business based on *real data*. You can save money by catching things like duplicate subscriptions, bank errors, and checks you thought made it to the bank but only made it to the bottom of your purse. It allows you to set realistic goals around your income and know which of your products or services are profitable and which are not. It saves you time and tons of stress when it comes time to file your taxes. I could go on and on about the benefits, but I am pretty sure you get the picture.

But the biggest difference bookkeeping can make is the way it can **transform how you feel about money. Every time you remove stress around your money, you are transforming your relationship with money for the better.** Every time you interact consciously with money, your relationship shifts in the right direction. After working intimately with over 100 people and their money, I can tell you that the better your relationship is with money, the better you are at attracting it, receiving it, and experiencing true abundance.

This isn't just about business either. These truths around tracking your money apply to your personal accounts as well.

FAQs About Hiring a Bookkeeper

I'm too small or too disorganized. Won't they judge me?

I can only speak for myself, but I see hundreds of bank accounts each month, and within these accounts are often hundreds, if not thousands, of transactions. Honestly, I don't really think about a single transaction, or even a group of transactions, enough to make a judgment. Some accounts have millions of dollars, some are pulling from overdraft. My job is to balance your books, not judge how you manage your money. No matter where you are, you need to start somewhere, and chances are your bookkeeper has seen it all. I personally love helping someone who is really disorganized or just starting out. It is part of what brings me joy. I love taking something that is completely messy and turning it into a well-oiled machine. It's like a giant puzzle to be solved. There is no such thing in my book as "too small" or "too disorganized."

When should I hire a bookkeeper?

You should hire a bookkeeper as soon as you are feeling like your books are too big a project for you to handle on your own, or you simply want to spend your time doing other things that generate income. If bookkeeping is the last thing on your list and you avoid your books because you dread doing them, it might be time to find help. Lots of people beat themselves up, saying: "How hard can it be?" or "I should know how to do this." Stop feeling guilty and judging yourself. Life is too short to do things you hate doing. And, with the right team or the right training and the right systems in place, you might find you actually *enjoy* looking at your numbers.

How do I find the right person?
Ask around and get recommendations from business buddies, friends, family or networking groups. Make a couple of phone calls and see who clicks. You are going to be sharing some pretty intimate details with this person, so you want to feel comfortable talking with them. Also, make sure the person you are about to hire is detail-oriented and don't be afraid to ask for references. Keep in mind many bookkeepers work remotely. I have lots of clients I have never even met face to face. Just about everything can be done over the phone or through email.

(**Shameless plug:** I hear All the Details Consulting is pretty awesome. Check out www.all-details.com to learn more and to get in touch with me!)

Isn't it expensive to hire a bookkeeper?
Well, what is it costing you to *not* have a bookkeeper? Bookkeepers often save you money by helping you discover things like duplicate or unnecessary subscriptions, bank errors, and client payments that were never received, not to mention time that could be spent making more money.

Not sure where to start? I've got you covered. And just like my tagline I used when I first started networking, I can help you get your shit together!

How to Get Your $hit Together
The Nine Things I Wish Every Bookkeeping Client Knew About Money

1. Keep your business and personal money separate

My #1 suggestion is to maintain separate bank accounts for your business and personal money. I am often surprised at how many people don't know this. And, seriously, no judgment if you currently don't have separate bank accounts.

Here's why it's important: Having separate bank accounts makes it much easier to do your bookkeeping and see your numbers. Business owners are required to track all income and expenses for taxes. If you keep your accounts separate, you only need to track the transactions in and out of the business accounts.

This goes for checking, savings, credit cards, PayPal and any other type of account you may use. If you receive or spend money for your business, it should go in or out of accounts that are separate from your personal accounts.

If you use the same account for business and personal, it is difficult, if not impossible, to track which income and expenses are for business, and which are personal. You also run the risk of forgetting about charges you put on personal cards and losing out on potential deductions. Trust me, opening a separate business bank account is the *easiest* way to simplify your life if you are a business owner.

I have seen too many people struggle at the end of the year—poring through personal credit card and bank statements line by line, trying to remember what each purchase was for, and scrambling for tax deductions. Do yourself a huge favor and get separate accounts set up today. It will save you a tremendous amount of time, energy, and stress.

I get it—sometimes you don't have your business credit card with you, and you have to use a personal card, or vice versa. That's ok. Just make sure you make note of it when it happens, so you don't forget. Try not to make this a regular habit, but don't beat yourself up if you slip, either. If you are working with a bookkeeper or doing your own books, add it in when it happens so you can forget about it and move on. This way the transaction will be in your books at tax time. Easy peasy.

If you have personal expenses you want your business to cover, make a transfer from your business account into your personal account in one lump sum and pay for the items from your personal account. No need to have your daughter's soccer fees on your business books. When you make a transfer from your business account to a personal account this is called an *owner's draw* or *owner's distribution* and it is part of your equity in your company. It does not impact the profit and loss (aka your profitability or bottom line).

If you need to invest personal money into your business to pay for expenses, make a transfer for the total amount you need and then pay the expenses out of the business account. This way the detail of the expenses will be tracked in your business account. This type of transaction is called an *owner's investment* or *owner's contribution* and is also considered part of your equity in your business.

So why is having separate accounts so important? From a legal standpoint, it helps keep you and your business separate. When I first opened my company, I had a lawyer walk me through the steps, just to make sure I was doing everything correctly. He gave me some great advice and some insight on why this is so important. Have you heard the term "piercing the corporate veil"? I had heard it before but didn't really know what it meant.

He explained if you are set up as an LLC or a corporation, these are legal entities that help protect your personal assets from business assets. If you were to get sued, the legal structure is in place so you don't lose everything in both your business and your personal life. One of the first things lawyers will do to determine if you in fact are a different entity from your business is look at your finances. If you operate your personal life out of the same bank accounts as your business, they can disregard your legal structure and you no longer have the legal protection that keeps your business and personal life separate. YIKES!

If the idea of setting up separate accounts stresses you out, take it in baby steps. Maybe start with a checking account one month and then add a credit card account the next. Setting up a business account is relatively simple. You just need to provide the bank with a few documents—similar to what you would need to provide if you were setting up a personal account—and you will be on your way to more financial simplicity.

More importantly, setting up a business account shows the Universe (and your clients and vendors) you are serious about making money as an entrepreneur.

2. Make it easy for people to give you money (and easy for you to receive money)

This seems like an obvious one, but almost every single business owner I have worked with has some hang-up or other that is blocking their clients from giving them money.

Things like a broken link on their website so people aren't able to pay them, an inability to tell people what they do and how potential clients can work with them, or no system for tracking who owes them money, so invoices don't get sent. It seems kind of crazy looking at it from the outside, but when you are in the middle of the day-to-day of running a business, so many things can slip through the cracks. Making it easy for people to give you money often ends up being one of those things.

When I first started my business, I was charging my clients an hourly rate. Part of this was because it was hard to know how much time a project would actually take. I was worried that I would underprice or overprice my time. What I didn't realize is how much time it would take to *track my time*. As my business grew and I added more and more clients to the mix it became even more complicated.

I started by tracking my time on a spreadsheet and then eventually moved to an app. Because I was constantly on the go and working on multiple clients every day, I would keep a sticky note handy to track 15 minutes here, 30 minutes there. I would spend the last part of my day—usually at 8:00 pm on the couch deciphering my notes on this tiny little sticky note I had made throughout the day to get things entered into my app.

At the end of the month, I would add up all the time I spent for each customer and transfer all of this information into an invoice template and email it to the customer. I would then transfer all of this information over to my accounting software to track the total of who owed me. Essentially, I was using three different systems to manage my time tracking and invoicing. It was completely inefficient and literally took me a full day each month to get my invoicing done, not to mention the 15 to 30 minutes (or more) I would spend each day tracking my time. I would then have to wait weeks, and sometimes longer for clients to mail checks.

I was resisting setting up systems that supported money coming to me with ease. I kept telling myself a story that I didn't have time to stop and do the analysis, research and leg work it was going to take to get a more efficient system in place.

When I finally transformed my business and took a long hard look at my systems and structures, it completely changed the way I did business. While it didn't change overnight and it was a little scary to take the leap, I moved all of my clients to retainers, put contracts in place to better define expectations and offer more protection, and got everyone set up on automatic payments. This was life changing. I gained back a few valuable days each month that I could now spend on growing my business, and even more valuable—some much-needed personal time.

All of my retainers are set up for the payment to process on the 5th of the month so I am paid before I do the work. This helps my clients with their monthly budgets because they know exactly what to expect each month, and I know how much will be coming in. It also helps protect me from clients who might default on payments. Yes, I still analyze how much time I spend on a client project, but it is from a much more objective place rather than minute by minute.

I am now doing a lot less busy work and getting paid more. Isn't that everyone's goal?

Payments are set up to process automatically. I go to bed on the 4th of the month and wake up the morning of the 5th with several thousand dollars sitting in my bank account. All of the retainers are automated, so I don't have to think about sending an invoice to a client, collecting their funds, or going to the bank to deposit a check. Overnight, the money fairies process each of my clients' credit cards, and voila! A few days' worth of work done while I sleep. Ahhhhh... the wonders of the modern world. I seriously LOVE this part.

Depending on what you sell, make sure you have "pay now" links and make it easy for people to send you money. It might be a PayPal link or a pay now button through your QuickBooks invoicing.

Don't stress about the amount you are paying in merchant fees. Merchant fees are a cost of doing business. If you want to easily collect money and have it automatically go into your account rather than wait for a check (that may or may not show up) and deal with the hassle of paper checks, accepting credit cards is a no-brainer. If the thought of paying for merchant fees stresses you out, raise your rates just a tad to cover the expense.

I see so many people spend hours and hours of time trying to get the best rate for merchant fees. And while yes, it is always good to save money, many times you are tripping over a dollar to save a dime. Unless you are doing a huge volume in sales, the amount you will save usually is not worth the time and energy investment to research and change merchant accounts. What is perhaps more critical is the ease in which people can pay you and keeping your point of sale system easy for both your customers and tracking your income once it comes into your account.

If you think you don't have time to look at your systems, you may want to think about what you are losing by not having these systems in place. Spend some time working *on* the business instead of *in* the business. It will pay off tremendously in both time and profits.

3. Have a system to track who owes you money

This is another one that seems obvious when you are simply talking about business, but it can get pretty complicated quickly without the right structure in place. One of the most useful structures you can have is an effective and easy system that tracks who owes you money, how much they owe you, and when payments are made (whether that is in full or partial payments).

So many business owners focus so much of their energy on marketing and *getting* the clients, but once the client has agreed to a service, it unravels on the back end.

One of my bookkeeping clients works with a vendor who is a textbook case of poor systems around receiving money. I have worked with this client for several years and I wonder how this particular vendor is still in business with the amount of money they leave on the table. Because they provide an ongoing service that is part of the monthly expense for my client, I always check to make sure we have the bill recorded each month so my client's month end numbers are accurate. It is not unusual for the vendor to go months without sending an invoice. There are many times we have to email them and ask them for an invoice. What's even worse is after we have given them approval to charge the card on file, sometimes they don't process the payment.

Another client has always had an issue with cash flow and finds it hard to get everything done in the day as most entrepreneurs often do. She runs a day spa and contracts with a couple of hotels to manage the on-property spa. Guests are allowed to put the service on their room. In order for her to get paid for the massages that are put on room charge, she needs to invoice the hotel. When I took over invoicing for her, she had no system in place to track what was already invoiced and what had been paid. Based on the quantity of services provided, this needed to happen on a weekly basis. Her cash flow to pay her therapists depended on getting paid from the service she was providing to her customers.

So many of my clients struggle with this piece and it is so important! What is the use of working to get the clients and provide the service if you don't get paid!

QuickBooks or other financial software can help streamline this process tremendously. Even if you think you are too small, or your business isn't complicated enough to warrant a full-blown system, be sure you are setting yourself up for growth.

When I first started my business, I had these very same thoughts. I've told you how I tracked my hours on a spreadsheet. At the end of the month I would add up my hours for each client, multiply it by my hourly rate and send an invoice. When I received a check, I would mark it as paid on the spreadsheet. While it worked, it certainly was not efficient and as I added more clients it became increasingly difficult to track.

4. Do a little at a time and be consistent
Some people are so overwhelmed they don't know where to start with bookkeeping. The key is to *just start*. Start small, and with what feels easiest to you. Take the task at hand and break it down into manageable pieces. Maybe it's looking at your bank account every morning or committing to Financial Fridays where you update your books on Friday mornings, or Wealth Wednesdays where you review your reports on the first Wednesday of every month. Whatever it is, each time you make a choice to take a baby step in understanding and organizing your finances, you are one step closer to being empowered around money.

Be honest with yourself about what you can take on, and what you *want* to take on. I have set up QuickBooks files for clients who want to do it themselves and then *nothing* happens, I mean nothing. They think *How hard can it be? I can find the time for this*. But then months and months later (usually around January or February when a tax deadline is looming) I get an email or a call. They are usually stressed out and panicked because they need to get a full year of bookkeeping done within a matter of weeks. While this certainly can be done, it is not the easy or stress-free way to financial freedom.

The best bookkeeping results come from having a system and process where your books are shown some love and attention on a regular basis. This system might be done by you or by someone else, but the key is to be *regular*. **Do it daily, weekly, or monthly so you aren't in a panic on April 14.**

So here is my suggestion of what to do when. These can be done by you or your bookkeeper. It is totally ok to split up the tasks and take on only what you want to do.

Daily or Weekly
- **Look at your bank balances and transactions.** Get used to seeing the numbers on the screen. If you are one of those people who likes to ignore your money altogether, this is a great place to start. Look for anything that surprises you—good or bad. Maybe you see a transaction that you didn't know was on autopay, or maybe you are pleased to see that the client who is 60 days late finally paid their bill online. Looking at your bank account helps you keep your finger on the pulse of what is happening.

- **Enter transactions into your books**. It is way easier to remember what things are for if you look at them when they happen.

- **Record payments when you receive them**. If you get a check in the mail, don't deposit it until you enter it received in your books. But don't wait for weeks or months to deposit it, either!!! Don't risk forgetting if they paid you or not. Nothing is worse than not knowing if a client has paid you or asking a client for a check they have already given you. If you work with a bookkeeper either send a copy of the check, save the check stub, or communicate in some way the funds have been received. Maybe I'm crazy— when I get a check in the mail I feel a huge sense of satisfaction in running back from the mail box, ripping open the envelope and jumping on my laptop to enter the payment. Receiving money is one of the best parts of owning a business. *This is the fun part!*

- **Invoice every week or at a minimum every month.** Better yet, automate your process so money comes to you at regular intervals (see #2 and #3 for more on this).

Monthly
- **Reconcile your books to your bank statements**. I live to balance to the penny. Most people cringe at the very thought. Reconciling is the act of comparing what is in your books to what actually happened in your bank account. In theory, these should be the same. If they aren't, something is not accurate and 97 percent of the time, it is something in your books, not a bank error. It might be you transposed a number or you might have entered something twice. The key is to find these little mistakes to make sure your books are accurate. I once took on a new bookkeeping client only to find the previous bookkeeper had forgotten to enter a $10,000 check several months earlier and never bothered to reconcile. Whoops! If I had not reconciled the account, my client would have thought she had $10K more in the bank than she really did. While this is an extreme example, you get the idea.

- **Review your numbers.** Look at a profit and loss and maybe even a balance sheet. Compare numbers to previous periods. Is there a reason you are making more this month than last? Keep it up! Is there a reason your expenses are more from last year at this same time? If you aren't sure, it might be worth looking into. If this feels overwhelming, just start by looking at your income. A few key terms in case you aren't sure:

○ A **profit and loss statement** (P & L) shows how much income you have brought in through sales as well as how much you have spent. If you subtract your income from your expenses, that gives you the profit (or loss) for that particular period.

○ A **balance sheet** shows what your business is worth. It includes your assets—things like money you have in your bank account, vehicles, and other property you own, as well as your liabilities—things like your credit card debt, or loans. It also shows your personal equity—what you have put in or taken out of the business.

○ You can run reports two different ways.
  ▪ A **cash report** is what is physically in the bank—money you have received from clients and bills you have paid.
  ▪ An **accrual report** is what has been invoiced but not necessarily received. It also includes bills that have been sent to you, but not necessarily paid.

• **Review and answer any questions about transactions.** If you are working with a bookkeeper, review the questions they send you every month. If you are doing bookkeeping on your own, look at your transactions for the month and make sure everything is in the right place.

Quarterly
- **Do more of the same**. If you don't reconcile your bank statements monthly, be sure to do them at least quarterly.

- **Compare your numbers**. The start of a new quarter is a great time to look at the previous period in comparison including overall income, overall expenses and overall profit. Look for trends and if you see something you don't understand, start looking for answers. This is also a good time to look for money leaks.

- **Touch base with your CPA**. It is always good to touch base with the person who will be doing your taxes about any changes or shifts in your business on a quarterly basis; that way you aren't surprised come tax time when your bill is higher than you thought or you find out you could have structured something a different way and saved a ton of money. Use the experts you have on your team regularly.

Yearly
- **Get your taxes done.** 'nuff said.

- **Set goals for the next year.** Look at numbers in November and again in January. Are you where you want to be? If not, what is a realistic and obtainable goal? This can be the number of clients you have, the amount of income you want to generate, the amount of profit you want to make in either a dollar amount or a percentage, or even saving money in a certain area. No goal is too big or too small.

- **Look for where you made money.** I love to spend some time at the end of each year really looking at what I offer and determining if the offerings were profitable. Sometimes you might find that the main thing you offer doesn't make you much money, but another product you haven't really focused on is a goldmine waiting to be tapped.

- **Look for where you could have saved money in expenses.** Are there areas where you are over-spending? Do you pay for subscriptions for things you don't use? Cancel them. Can you find less expensive vendors who offer similar services? Make the switch.

- **Look at things you've invested in that are not likely to happen again.** As you are looking at your overall numbers for the year, acknowledge items that are one-time things. Maybe you invested in a new website, or you took a class, or hired a coach to help you grow your business. All of these things may have decreased your overall profit for the year but aren't likely to be an expense for the next year. (Don't forget to budget for these types of upgrades each year. Investing in your business is important!)

- **Set a budget if you feel so inclined,** or at least a money map. I usually map out my numbers month by month, once a year. I plug in all of my offerings, how many clients I want to attract each month, and the rate they will pay me. This helps me to under-stand how and when cash will be coming into my business. I don't really consider it a budget because I don't use it to compare my actual numbers to my budget and look at the variance. But I do use it to help me set some income goals and also figure out how I want to invest in my business and where I want to focus my energy.

Just a note: Please don't panic. I understand that this list can be completely overwhelming—especially if you don't have any or many systems in place. It is totally ok to start where you are and pick one or two things you want to focus on at a time. Remember: baby steps.

Take it easy on yourself but don't bury your head in the sand, either. Like all good things, transforming your relationship with money takes diligence and time.

5. Have systems, processes and structures that support you YOUR WAY

So many of my new clients are frozen in fear around money when we begin to work together. They aren't sure where to start and feel overwhelmed. Sometimes it is fear of the unknown, sometimes it is fear of not doing the "right" thing, and sometimes the fear is a result of money stories and beliefs.

My antidote for fear is to create a system that works for you and supports you.

Systems are the tools behind your habits.

Systems are key to bringing you one step closer to understanding your numbers.

Systems make it easier for you to live in harmony with money.

Systems provide a container for your money to flow.

Systems help you declutter around money.

Systems help reduce your stress and confusion around money.

The bottom line is once you have a process set up, it helps everything run like clockwork. In turn, this helps reduce stress and negative feelings around money. And focusing on the positive rather than the negative attracts abundance.

Creating systems and healthy habits supports a shift from fear to knowledge which, in turn, empowers you around money and makes your life easier.

I could write an entire book around systems, so this list just scratches the surface, but here are a few tips to consider when setting up systems.

Have a process that works for you. Money systems are not one-size-fits-all. And I am not here to give you a 10-step formula that will solve all your money problems. Systems that work for me might not work for you.

Set up your books in a way that gives you the information you need. Not all businesses are the same, and not every business owner wants or needs the same information. When you are setting up your books, make sure it will give you the reports you want. If it doesn't, do a little tweaking (and don't be afraid to ask a seasoned bookkeeper to help you come up with the right structure so you can pull the information you want). So many people think that book-keeping is all black and white—and while that might be true in the actual balancing of your books, the way your books are structured is completely customizable.

Make it fun. Create processes and rituals around looking at your money. Eat chocolate, do your financials sitting outside at your patio table overlooking your pool with a beer in hand. Do whatever it takes to make it feel like less of a chore and more of a reward. Big shout-out to Bari Tessler here. If you want to create some beautiful money practices, I highly recommend her blog or her book, *The Art of Money*.

Use your own language. When you are looking at your reports, you should be able to understand what every line item means. When I first started my bookkeeping business, I had a client whose CPA assigned every single category a number. While this is not unusual in the financial world, the reports were generated with just the number and no de-scription. Whenever they looked at their profit and loss statements, they had to refer back to the chart of numbers just to decipher the category. Talk about unnecessary confusion!

I am a huge fan of using your own language within your set of books. Make it mirror the language you use in your day-to-day business. Are you a massage therapist? Maybe you breakdown your income into massages, facials, and body treatments. You don't need to use general terms like "sales and services" unless that is what you want to use. And don't be afraid to make it personal—they are *your* books, after all.

As I work with my clients, I always have questions each month about how to categorize a few transactions. Typically, these get categorized into the "ask my client" account. I send the list to my client; they send me answers back, and I get them categorized into the right place. One of my clients loves to refer to these as the WTFs, and so it stuck. If you open up their QuickBooks and look at the chart of accounts, you will see a category called WTF. Simply perfect! Another client is a unicorn CEO (she seriously is magic!) and her labor is coded as unicorn squad in her books. **Be creative. Make it work for you.**

Simplify your chart of accounts so you can understand what is happening in your books and use a language that makes sense to you. If certain terms stress you out or make you feel guilty, change them. Feel guilty about your credit card debt that you have from a class or program you took? Change it to "Investment in my future." As long as the terminology makes sense to you, and you are able to translate your language as needed to the person who is doing your taxes (and who BTW only sees your books once a year for a couple of hours, so no big deal), then go for it. Make it your own.

Start small and start where you are. If you are new to bookkeeping, don't start with complicated systems like job costing and tracking inventory. Start with the basics and add in layers as you go along. You may find that some of the more complicated tracking features aren't really needed.

Have a team and ask for help when you need it. (see #6 for more on this).

Have a system for your income. (see #2 and #3).

Have a system for your receipts and expenses. This can be *very* simple—especially considering how digital the world has become. My system for receipts is about as simple as it gets—when I go out to lunch with someone, I write their name and the purpose for the meeting on the receipt. I come home and put it in a file titled "receipts" and it includes everything for the entire tax year. That's it. I don't separate it by client, or file by month (although if you have lots of transactions, monthly is a good option). The rest of the details are downloaded into my books with the financial software that I use. I might put some notes in the memo of my transaction in QuickBooks if needed, but for the most part that pretty much covers it. Very rarely do I ever go back and look at receipts, but I do keep them just in case the IRS wants to look at them. If you want to go completely paperless, many software systems are now incorporating image attachment to the functionality. This allows you to take a photo of your receipt, attach the image to the transaction and then throw the receipt away.

6. It's OK to ask for help
What happens if you get a system in place to make sense of your numbers and you don't understand how to read them, or what they mean? You don't have to do this alone and if you don't like doing it, that's ok!

If you are feeling overwhelmed with the money aspect of your business, hire someone (or a team of people) to help you. They can help make your life easier in so many ways and you can hire out pieces; it doesn't have to be all or nothing. Your financial team can be as big or as small as you need, and they can do just one or two tasks or do lots of things for you depending on what you need and your comfort level with your finances. They can be a coach and a cheerleader and hold you accountable.

One of my favorite clients paid me the biggest compliment when she said, "I would be in jail if it weren't for you." After laughing hysterically for a few minutes, I paused to think about how many other clients might feel this same way. I get it. Paying attention to paperwork and opening bills isn't everybody's jam. If you are someone who avoids numbers like the plague, a bookkeeper can keep track of the details that keep you out of jail.

So, let me break down your options:

To recap, a **bookkeeper** is someone who helps you track all of the transactions that happen in your business. This person may also help you with other things related to finances like payroll, sales tax, invoicing, receiving payments, and paying bills. Out of everyone on your financial team, you will probably interact with this person the most.

An **accountant** is someone who often has a degree and/or is a CPA which stands for Certified Public Accountant. Accountants do lots of different things including taxes, audits, and financial reporting. Their education level is significantly higher than a bookkeeper and so is their price tag.

While there are lots of people out there who are both accountants and bookkeepers, it is important to understand the differences in these two roles. While accountants *can* do bookkeeping, it usually is not their specialty and they typically will charge more than an average bookkeeper for the same service. No offense to my favorite CPAs, but in my experience, they usually aren't the best bookkeepers because they don't do it all the time.

You don't need to hire a CPA to do your taxes, but there are certainly huge financial benefits in working with someone who knows their stuff. The important thing is to make sure the person doing your taxes understands your business and knows tax strategy. Don't hire someone who just does personal taxes to do your business taxes. Not all accountants and CPAs focus on taxes, so be sure to look for someone who specializes.

If your taxes aren't complicated, you can also go with a simple tax preparer; some bookkeepers will take this on, but a word of advice: good tax strategists are worth their weight in gold. Taxes can be extremely complicated to navigate and there are certain strategies with how your business is structured and how you pay yourself that will impact the amount of tax you owe. It is always good to have an ongoing relationship with a tax accountant so you are strategizing and planning all year long, not just on April 15th when it is too late.

Your bookkeeper and tax accountant should communicate when something comes up that will impact your taxes. If you make a big purchase or restructure how you are doing

THE LAND OF PLENTY

business, it is a good idea to keep these two people in the loop.

Any time something big comes up with my clients, I simply send the tax accountant a quick email to confirm how this should be entered in the books. It makes it much easier to handle these on a case-by-case basis as they happen rather than sending a long list of questions at the end of the year when your tax accountant is super busy dealing with every-one else's questions and tax returns.

Bookkeepers and tax accountants can save you money, time, and stress. Imagine next April 15. You sleep in, sip coffee, read a book, or go to a movie... *because your taxes were done in February!* Dreamy!

In addition to an accountant and bookkeeper, you may also want to have a **financial planner**—which is someone who helps you look at long-term goals. They typically focus on your retirement accounts and exit planning to help you project what you need to earn and save to meet your goals.

Another person you might want on your team is a **financial coach**. They can help you develop habits, understand money management, and help you set and achieve short and long-term money goals.

7. Invest in the things that save you time and money

I see two common types of people in business: those who overspend and don't pay attention to where their money goes and those who are overly concerned about where every penny is spent. If you are a penny pincher (aka Saving Energy from the Money Mojo quiz) this section is for you.

Let me say this loud and proud—don't be afraid to invest in the things that save you time or money! You could **invest in software and systems** like QuickBooks, a point of sale system, or a task management system. You could also **invest in team members** who get things done more effi-ciently than you ever could.

The sooner you get these systems in place, the better. A couple of years ago I had a client who was just opening a new business. He spent a few months doing research, setting up a point of sale system, getting bookkeeping and payroll set up and making sure it all worked seamlessly before he opened his doors. The results were phenomenal. Within a few months he had more than exceeded his initial revenue goals. He was able to see exactly what was going on in his business from the very beginning. I have no doubt some of his success can be linked to his investment in systems that allowed him to focus on growth rather than trying to figure it all out and winging it as he went along.

In comparison, I have another client who has been in business for over a decade. She still struggles with some very basic systems, and her numbers show it. She has past-due clients who often never pay, and she is always struggling with cash flow because she doesn't have a system in place for receiving money when she makes a sale and collecting from her clients. She lacks a system for tracking and follow-up.

Systems save you time and money in the long run. Get it set up now instead of later before it gets more complicated. It is better to have a system with more bells and whistles than you need so you can grow into it than no system at all.

Think long term. Taking the leap to spend the money can be a stretch, but believe me, investments are worth it!

Don't be afraid to **invest in yourself through education and coaching**. Investing in a coach was the best thing I have ever done for my business. It allowed me to see growth opportunities I would have never seen otherwise and gave me the structure I needed to create a sustainable business. Investments helped me build a business that I love—one that doesn't burn me out and gives me lots money *and* lots of space to enjoy life.

Time is money, especially when you are an entrepreneur. If you can charge a client $50 an hour, then anything that you can hire out for less than $50 an hour should be a no-brainer. Invest in things like housekeeping, landscaping, and errands that are easily outsourced, not to mention how awesome it is to come home to a clean house or not spend a Saturday pulling weeds. **If you don't have enough time in the day to get through your task list, spend your time doing the things that will generate money**. Keep in mind—it's not just the money. If you are trying to do it all, what is this costing you? Your health, your relationships, your family time?

8. Know your numbers
Look at your numbers at least every quarter, if not every month—this includes your income and expenses. Money empowerment begins with knowledge. (See #4 for what to do when.)

The first time I met Shannon, she was a speaker at a marketing conference I attended. She told a story of how she became an entrepreneur. While working as a public school teacher in New York City, she commuted several hours each day back and forth to work. She also had a business on the side, hand-making invitations for weddings and parties. Being great at marketing and good at what she did, her business grew by leaps and bounds. While the growth was great, she was working all the time, and ex-hausted. When the end of the year came around, Shannon turned in all of her receipts and paperwork to her tax preparer. She had no idea how much money she had coming in, and how much she had in expenses. Imagine her surprise when she got a call from her preparer to let her know that she had made a whopping $12 profit.

She told this story to illustrate how marketing grew her business, but I love how it reminds us why It is so important to know your numbers. Do you think she would have busted her ass to hand-make all of those cards and painstakingly tie hundreds of ribbons for a mere $12? Absolutely not!

When you know your numbers, you can make empowered and educated decisions about what you should keep doing in your business, and what you should stop doing. If you realize a product you are offering is not making you money, or is even causing you to lose money, knowing this information gives you the power to make a shift so you can become profitable.

9. Be a good steward of your money

It is soooo important to be friends with your money. Give your money a good, happy home. Make sure you have a good relationship with your money and treat it like a good friend. Don't bury your head in the sand, ignore it or constantly be angry with it. Treat your money with respect and love. Your money mindset makes a huge difference. Be grateful for what you have. The energy you have around your money will reflect back to you in your bank account and your ability to enjoy the money you have.

Some Additional Advice

Take a deep breath. You don't have to do all of this today, or this month or even this year. Start small. What is the one thing you think would make the most difference in your business? Do what speaks to you the most. The important thing is not to be stalled in fear. **Pick just one**. I promise it will be easier than you think, and the long-term benefits will be well worth the effort. Once you feel comfortable with the first change you can move on to the next. Don't let this opportunity pass you by and do nothing. Commit right now to take your first baby step towards transformation.

> *The journey of a thousand miles*
> *begins with one step.*
> *– Lao Tzu*

Be gentle with yourself

If you have been avoiding money most of your adult life, or you have told yourself a story that you aren't good with money, starting new habits around money can be scary. It is ok to take a break, go for a walk, and come back to it when you are ready. There may be some deep-seated fears that need to be addressed. Give yourself the space and time to let it all sink in and incorporate your new relationship with money. Forgive yourself for any past mistakes you made around money. Carrying this kind of baggage isn't doing you any good. Give yourself a break and stop judging yourself for debt, ignorance, or whatever money shame you are carrying around. Many people don't even have the courage to pick up a book like this, so kudos for starting!

It's ok to be imperfect (said by this perfectionist book-keeper)

I totally admit that I am a perfectionist. When someone asks me to describe myself, I love to respond like Mary Poppins, "I'm practically perfect in every way." While some might see my perfectionism as a flaw, I have learned to use this to my advantage in my business.

HOWEVER, there are lots of people out there who hide behind perfectionism as the reason not to complete, launch or even start a project and I'll be the first to admit I suffer from this "perfectionismitus" at times.

When it comes to looking at your numbers, setting up systems that support you, or even finding a team to have your back around money, the motto here should be *Just Do It*. Numbers don't need to be scary. The more you avoid them, the more stories you can and will make up about how horrible they are, or how you aren't good with money, or why you will never understand your numbers because you aren't good at math. Let me be real here. These are all *stories*. Stories that you have picked up somewhere along the way and these stories aren't serving you. Start small. Allow yourself to be imperfect because imperfect is better than not at all.

And honestly, what is it costing you to not know your numbers and not be organized?

Money Breakthrough Questions

Which of these actions are your going to start doing *today*? Write it down and commit. (Hint: If you don't have separate bank accounts—do this one *today*.)

What systems would be most helpful for you right now?

Where do you need support?

What have you been avoiding?

What systems can you implement that would save you time or money or both? Why do you think you are resisting or avoiding setting these systems up?

Resources to Help You Live in the Land of Plenty

I am excited to share this list of amazing authors and money empowerment leaders with you. While this is in no way a comprehensive list of all the books and authors out there who are talking about money empowerment and consciousness around money, these are some of my favorites and a great place to start.

Denise Duffield-Thomas
As you already know, I am a huge fan of Denise. Her approach to money mindset work is top in the field. If you want to see change around your ability to manifest money, she is the best.

- *Chillpreneur: The New Rules for Creating Success, Freedom, and Abundance on Your Terms*
- *Get Rich, Lucky Bitch!: Release Your Money Blocks and Live a First-Class Life*
- *Lucky Bitch: A Guide for Exceptional Women to Create Outrageous Success*

Chillpreneur is my favorite as it has lots of great advice on running a business in a way that supports you.

Denise's Money Bootcamp is phenomenal and the accompanying Facebook group is one of the most supportive and loving environments you can find for money mindset work. It's not cheap but it is well worth the investment. Check it out at www.denisedt.com, and at the very least, join her email list and/or follow her on social media. She always has something down to earth to say about money.

Lynne Twist
The Soul of Money: Reclaiming the Wealth of Our Inner Resources

As I mentioned, this is probably my favorite book on understanding money on a deep soul level. Beautiful heart-felt stories from people of every wealth status and every corner of the earth brought tears to my eyes. This is one of the most moving books on money you will ever read. Don't miss Lynne's interview with Oprah on Super Soul Sunday.

Bari Tessler
The Art of Money: A Life-Changing Guide to Financial Happiness

Bari has a similar approach to money as I do, maybe because she was also a bookkeeper, and in this great read, she talks about both the practical how-tos and the money mindset side of things. She also offers a year-long money course called the Art of Money and her blog posts are thought-provoking and right on point.

Jen Sincero
You are a BADASS at Making Money: Mastering the Mindset of Wealth

Jen has the best sense of humor and will have you laughing hysterically as you read. She keeps it real and to the point and truly inspires you to live your best life. A must-read.

Steve Jobs
Love What You Do Stanford Graduation Speech

To read the entire text or watch a video of Steve Jobs delivering his Love What You Do graduation speech go to: https://news.stanford.edu/2005/06/14/jobs-061505/

Elizabeth Gilbert
Big Magic: Creative Living Beyond Fear

It's hard to go wrong with Elizabeth Gilbert. This book talks about creativity and where it comes from. While it isn't about money, it's all about living a magical life full of joy and possibility.

Gay Hendricks
The Big Leap: Conquer Your Hidden Fear and Take Life to the Next Level

This book was life-changing for me. It is all about working in your Zone of Genius rather than your Zone of Excellence. He also talks about hitting your upper limits and how to move past them. If you want to level up your life, read this book.

Danielle LaPorte
The Desire Map: A Guide to Creating Goals with Soul

Desire Mapping is an amazing process and helps you set goals based on how you want to *feel* rather than setting an arbitrary goal that may leave you feeling unsatisfied and empty when you achieve it. Desire Mapping has been an incredibly valuable tool in my journey. In addition to the book, trained facilitators teach workshops around *The Desire Map.*

Sheryl Sandberg
Lean In: Women, Work, and the Will to Lead

A must-read for any woman in the corporate world. This was one of the first books I read about women and the workplace and it helped inspire me as I was breaking out of the Matrix.

Mike Michalowicz
Clockwork: Design Your Business to Run Itself

A great book about setting up your systems in your business so you can have a life again. Lots of practical advice. Mike is also the author of *Profit First: Transform Your Business from a Cash-Eating Monster to a Money-Making Machine* among other great books for entrepreneurs. While I don't have the time to get into the details of *Profit First* here, it is a good system for some entrepreneurs to manage cash flow. Like all systems, it is not for everyone, but it has some very valuable insights and viewpoints about paying yourself as a business owner and how to allocate money as it is received.

Money Empowerment Project®
I would love to have you be part of my money empowerment community! Check out my website for current offerings, take the Find Your Money Mojo Quiz, and get on my email list.
www.moneyempowermentproject.com

All the Details Consulting
If you are looking for a conscious bookkeeper to help you get your shit together, check out my website.
www.all-details.com

My Award Show Acceptance Speech (aka Acknowledgments)

This book would not have been possible without these people. From the bottom of my heart, the gratitude is overflowing.

Madeleine Eno for being my cheerleader.

Greta for crossing my t's and dotting my i's.

Jacqueline Morasco for being my energetic guide.

Angella Johnson for igniting my fire.

Priscilla Stephan for helping me discover my soul's work and purpose.

My grandfather Bill for pulling his angelic strings to align the stars.

Ginger Adams for helping me reconnect to my WHY.

My clients for trusting me and sharing their intimate details that were the inspiration for writing this book.

All the bold women who have stepped up and started the conversation around conscious money and money empowerment.

Above all, my husband Brian for being along for the ride and saying yes to living the dream.

CPSIA information can be obtained
at www.ICGtesting.com
Printed in the USA
FSHW010508221119
64293FS